First World War
and Army of Occupation
War Diary
France, Belgium and Germany

8 DIVISION
Divisional Troops
Anti-Aircraft Section
and Divisional Ammunition Column
9 September 1914 - 30 November 1914

WO95/1695

The Naval & Military Press Ltd
www.nmarchive.com
Published in association with The National Archives

Published by

The Naval & Military Press Ltd

Unit 10 Ridgewood Industrial Park,

Uckfield, East Sussex,

TN22 5QE England

Tel: +44 (0) 1825 749494

www.naval-military-press.com

www.nmarchive.com

This diary has been reprinted in facsimile from the original. Any imperfections are inevitably reproduced and the quality may fall short of modern type and cartographic standards.

© **Crown Copyright**
Images reproduced by permission of The National Archives, London, England, 2015.

Contents

Document type	Place/Title	Date From	Date To
Heading	1695 Divisional Ammunition Column Nov 1918 Diary Not Found		
Heading	8th Division 8th Divl Ammn Column Nov 1914-May 1919		
Heading	Ammunition Column 8th Division. Vol I. 4-30.11.14 May 1919		
War Diary	Hursley Camp	04/11/1914	04/11/1914
War Diary	Southampton	05/11/1914	05/11/1914
War Diary	Le Havre	06/11/1914	12/11/1914
War Diary	Merville	13/11/1914	13/11/1914
War Diary	Estaires	15/11/1914	30/11/1914
Heading	8th Divl. Ammn. Col. Vol I. 1-31.12.14		
War Diary	Estaires	01/12/1914	31/12/1914
Heading	8th, Division. 8th, D.A.C. January, 1915.		
Heading	8th Divl. Ammn. Col. Vol II 10-28.1.15		
War Diary	Estaires	10/01/1915	28/01/1915
Heading	8th, Division. 8th, D.A.C. February, 1915.		
Heading	8th Divl. Ammn. Col. Vol III 1-28.2.15		
War Diary	Estaires	01/02/1915	28/02/1915
War Diary		25/02/1915	28/02/1915
Heading	8th, Division. 8th, D.A.C. March, 1915.		
Heading	8th Divl. Ammn. Col. Vol IV 1-29.3.15		
War Diary	Merville	01/03/1915	29/03/1915
Heading	8th, Division. 8th, D.A.C. April, 1915.		
Heading	8th Divisional Ammn. Col. Vol V 5-29.4.15		
War Diary	Merville	05/04/1915	09/04/1915
War Diary	Estaires	17/04/1915	29/04/1915
Heading	8th, Division. 8th, D.A.C. May, 1915.		
Heading	8th Divl. Ammn. Col. Vol VI 4-31.5.15		
War Diary	N. of Estaires	04/05/1915	31/05/1915
Heading	8th, Division. 8th, D.A.C. June, 1915.		
Heading	8th Division 8th Divl. Ammn. Col Vol VII 5-28.6.15		
War Diary	N. Of Estaires	05/06/1915	28/06/1915
Heading	8th, Division. 8th, D.A.C. July, 1915.		
Heading	8th Division 8th Divl. Ammn. Coln Vol VIII 1-30-7-15		
War Diary	N. Of Estaires.	01/07/1915	30/07/1915
Heading	8th, Division. 8th, D.A.C. August, 1915.		
Heading	8th Division 8th Divl. Ammn. Coln Vol IX From 2 To 31.8.15		
War Diary	N. Of Estaires.	02/08/1915	31/08/1915
Heading	8th, Division. 8th, D.A.C. September, 1915.		
Heading	8th Division 8th Divl. Ammn. Coln Vol X Sept. 15		
War Diary	Doulieu.	02/09/1915	24/09/1915
War Diary	N. of Sailly	25/09/1915	29/09/1915
War Diary	Doulieu	30/09/1915	30/09/1915
Heading	8th, Division. 8th, D.A.C. October, 1915.		
Heading	8th Division 8th Divl. Ammn. Coln Vol XI Oct 15		
War Diary	Doulieu	02/10/1915	31/10/1915
Heading	8th, Division. 8th, D.A.C. November, 1915.		
Heading	8th Division 8th Divl. Ammn. Coln Nov. Vol XII		

War Diary	Doulieu	01/11/1915	30/11/1915
Heading	8th, Division. 8th, D.A.C. December, 1915.		
Heading	8th Divl. Ammn. Coln Dec. Vol XIII 121/7929		
War Diary	Doulieu	04/12/1915	20/12/1915
War Diary	Morbecque	21/12/1915	21/12/1915
War Diary	Roquetoire.	22/12/1915	22/12/1915
War Diary	Morbecque	23/12/1915	23/12/1915
War Diary	Doulieu	26/12/1915	26/12/1915
Heading	8th, Division. 8th, D.A.C. January, 1916.		
War Diary	Doulieu.	07/01/1916	30/01/1916
Heading	8th, Division. 8th, D.A.C. February, 1916.		
War Diary	Doulieu	01/02/1916	27/02/1916
Heading	8th, Division. 8th, D.A.C. March, 1916.		
War Diary	Doulieu	03/03/1916	30/03/1916
Heading	8th, Division. 8th. D.A.C. April, 1916.		
War Diary	Belloy	03/04/1916	22/04/1916
War Diary	Bavelincourt	28/04/1916	29/04/1916
Heading	8th, Division. 8th, D.A.C. May, 1916.		
War Diary	Bavelincourt	09/05/1916	17/05/1916
War Diary	Baisieux	17/05/1916	29/05/1916
Heading	8th, Division. 8th, D.A.C. June, 1916.		
War Diary	Baisieux	06/06/1915	17/06/1915
War Diary	Millencourt	14/06/1916	30/06/1916
Heading	I. Corps. First Army. Division Transferred From III. Corps, Fourth Army, 8.7.16. War Diary 8th Division Ammunition Column. July 1916		
Heading	A.G's Office Bde. Herewith War Diary For 8th Div. Am Column For Month Of July 1916		
War Diary	Millencourt	01/07/1916	04/07/1916
War Diary	Bavelincourt	05/07/1916	05/07/1916
War Diary	Crouy	06/07/1916	08/07/1916
War Diary	Auchel	08/07/1916	14/07/1916
War Diary	Nouveau Monde	15/07/1916	21/07/1916
War Diary	Annezin	22/07/1916	22/07/1916
War Diary	Verquigneul	24/07/1916	29/07/1916
Heading	8th, Division. 8th, D.A.C. August, 1916.		
Heading	Confidential. 8th Divisional Artillery. War Diary of 8th Div. Amm. Coln From 1-8-16 To 31-8-16 (Volume 21) With Appendices Nos. None		
War Diary	Verquigneul	01/08/1916	31/08/1916
Heading	8th, Division. 8th, D.A.C. September, 1916.		
Heading	Confidential. 8th Divisional Artillery. War Diary of 8th Division Amn Column From 1st Sept 1916 To 30 Sept 1916. (Volume) With Appendices Nos. None.		
War Diary	Verquigneul	01/09/1916	24/09/1916
Heading	8th, Division. 8th, D.A.C. October, 1916.		
Heading	Confidential. 8th Divisional Artillery. War Diary of 8th Div. Amn Coln. From 1-10-16 To 31-10-16 (Volume 21) With Appendices Nos		
War Diary	Verquigneul	12/10/1916	22/10/1916
War Diary	Labeuvriere	23/10/1916	23/10/1916
War Diary	Heuchin	24/10/1916	24/10/1916
War Diary	Etree Wamin	25/10/1916	25/10/1916
War Diary	Orville	26/10/1916	26/10/1916
War Diary	Talmas	27/10/1916	27/10/1916
War Diary	Daours	28/10/1916	31/10/1916

Heading	8th, Division. 8th, D.A.C. November, 1916.		
Heading	Confidential. 8th. Divisional Artillery War Diary of 8th Div. Am Coln From 1-11-16 To 30-11-16 (Volume) With Appendices Nos 2		
War Diary	Daours	01/11/1916	01/11/1916
War Diary	Carnoy	02/11/1916	28/11/1916
War Diary	Daours	29/11/1916	30/11/1916
Miscellaneous	Sent Up By 8th D.A.C.	25/11/1916	25/11/1916
Miscellaneous	Ammunition Sent To Guns By Wagon Lines Nov. 1st To Nov. 20th		
Miscellaneous	Officer Commanding, 8th Divisional Ammunition Column.	07/11/1916	07/11/1916
Miscellaneous		06/11/1916	06/11/1916
Heading	8th, Division. 8th, D.A.C. December, 1916.		
Heading	Confidential. 8th. Divisional Artillery War Diary of 8th Div. Am. Coln. From 1.12.16 To 31.12.16 (Volume XXVI) With Appendices Nos.		
War Diary	La Chaussee	01/12/1916	01/12/1916
War Diary	Andain Ville	03/12/1916	11/12/1916
War Diary	Bronfay Farm	12/12/1916	13/12/1916
War Diary	Bronfay Farm L4a.	14/12/1916	24/12/1916
War Diary	Bronfay Farm	26/12/1916	31/12/1916
Heading	Confidential. 8th. Divisional Artillery War Diary of 8 Div. Am. Col. From 1.1.17 To 31.1.17 (Volume 27) With Appendices Nos. None		
War Diary	Bronfay Farm	01/01/1917	13/01/1917
War Diary	Argueuvres	14/01/1917	22/01/1917
War Diary	Dromesnil	28/01/1917	30/01/1917
War Diary	Nr Goeuvres	31/01/1917	31/01/1917
Heading	Confidential. 8th Divisional Artillery. War Diary of 8th Div. Am. Col. From 1-2-17 To 28-2-17 (Volume XXVIII) With Appendices Nos.		
War Diary	Camp 117	01/02/1917	01/02/1917
War Diary	Bray	02/02/1917	26/02/1917
Heading	Confidential. 8th Divisional Artillery. War Diary of 8th Div. Am. Col. From 1-3-17 To 31-3-17 (Volume XXIX) With Appendices Nos.		
War Diary	Bray	02/03/1917	28/03/1917
War Diary	Allaines	28/03/1917	31/03/1917
Heading	Confidential. 8th Divisional Artillery War Diary of 8th Div. Am. Column From 1.4.17 To 30.4.17 (Volume 30) With Appendices Nos.		
War Diary	Allaines	01/04/1917	19/04/1917
War Diary	V.26.c	20/04/1917	21/04/1917
War Diary	V.26.c (57c)	21/04/1917	28/04/1917
War Diary	V.26.c	28/04/1917	29/04/1917
Heading	Confidential. 8th Divisional Artillery War Diary of 8th Div Am Column From 1-5-17 To 31-5-17 (Volume XXXI) With Appendices Nos.		
War Diary	V.26.3. (Nr Nurlu)	01/05/1917	17/05/1917
War Diary	V.26.e	18/05/1917	20/05/1917
War Diary	Camp 111	21/05/1917	22/05/1917
War Diary	Renescure	23/05/1917	25/05/1917
War Diary	Clairmarais	26/05/1917	31/05/1917

Heading	Confidential. 8th Divisional Artillery. War Diary Of 8th Div. Am. Column From 1st June 17 To 30th June 1917 (Volume XXXII) With Appendices Nos.		
War Diary	Clairmarais	04/06/1917	13/06/1917
War Diary	Caestre Area	13/06/1917	20/06/1917
War Diary	Poperinghe Area	20/06/1917	30/06/1917
Heading	Confidential. 8th Divisional Artillery. War Diary of 8th Divn Ammun Column From 1-7-17 To 30-7-17 (Volume XXXIII) With Appendices Nos.		
War Diary	Poperinghe Area	01/07/1917	30/07/1917
Heading	Confidential 8th Divisional Artillery. War Diary Of 8th Div Am Column From 31.7. To 31.8.17 (Volume 34) With Appendices Nos.		
War Diary	G.246.88	31/07/1917	06/08/1917
War Diary	Poperinghe	06/08/1917	29/08/1917
War Diary	Eecke Area	31/08/1917	01/09/1917
War Diary	Bailleul Area	02/09/1917	10/09/1917
War Diary	Nieppe	11/09/1917	29/09/1917
Miscellaneous	8th Divisional Artillery. Casualties that have Occurred In Personnel During Month Ending 30th September 1917 Appendix. A		
War Diary	Nieppe	02/10/1917	31/10/1917
Miscellaneous	8th Divisional Artillery. Casualties That Have Occurred In Personnel During Month Ending October 31st 1917 Appendix.		
War Diary	Nieppe	01/11/1917	15/11/1917
War Diary	Poperinghe	15/11/1917	30/11/1917
Miscellaneous	8th Divisional Artillery. Casualties That Have Occurred In Personnel During Month Ending November 30th 1917 Appendix		
War Diary	Poperinghe	01/12/1917	21/12/1917
War Diary	Oudezeele	25/12/1917	29/12/1917
War Diary	Vlamertinghe	01/01/1918	21/01/1918
War Diary	Poperinghe	24/01/1918	30/01/1918
Miscellaneous	8th Divisional Artillery. Casualties That Have Occurred In Personnel During Month Ending January 31st 1918. Appendix. A		
War Diary	Poperinghe	01/02/1918	28/02/1918
Heading	War Diary 8th Divisional Ammunition Column, R.A. March 1918		
War Diary	Vlamertinghe	01/03/1918	08/03/1918
War Diary	Poperinghe Elverdinghe Rd.	09/03/1918	22/03/1918
War Diary	Guillaucourt	23/03/1918	24/03/1918
War Diary	Caix	25/03/1918	25/03/1918
War Diary	Marcelcave Ignaucourt	26/03/1918	26/03/1918
War Diary	Ignaucourt	27/03/1918	27/03/1918
War Diary	Aubercourt	28/03/1918	28/03/1918
War Diary	Jumel	28/03/1918	28/03/1918
War Diary	Ailly Rouvrel Thezy	29/03/1918	29/03/1918
War Diary	St Nicholas	30/03/1918	31/03/1918
Miscellaneous	8th Divisional Artillery Casualties That Have Occurred In Personnel During Month Ending 31/3/18 Appendix. A.		
Miscellaneous	8th Divisional Ammunition Column Casualties That Have Occurred In Personnel During Month Ending 30 March 1918.	06/04/1918	06/04/1918

Heading	8th Divisional Artillery. 8th Divisional Ammunition Column R.F.A. April 1918.			
War Diary	St Nicholas		01/04/1918	04/04/1918
War Diary	Boves		04/04/1918	15/04/1918
War Diary	Vers		16/04/1918	17/04/1918
War Diary	Grandsart		17/04/1918	26/04/1918
War Diary	Grandsart March Erondelle		27/04/1918	30/04/1918
War Diary	Erondelles		01/05/1918	04/05/1918
War Diary	Erondelle Salouel		05/05/1918	07/05/1918
War Diary	Cuiry-House		08/05/1918	10/05/1918
War Diary	Cuiry House Les Venteaux		11/05/1918	11/05/1918
War Diary	Les Venteaux		12/05/1918	14/05/1918
War Diary	Les Grands Savarts		15/05/1918	27/05/1918
War Diary	Brevil Unchair		27/05/1918	27/05/1918
War Diary	Brevil Vendeuil		27/05/1918	27/05/1918
War Diary	Romain Vendeuil		27/05/1918	27/05/1918
War Diary	Les Grands Savarts		27/05/1918	27/05/1918
War Diary	Unchair Grugny		27/05/1918	27/05/1918
War Diary	Grugny Lhery		28/05/1918	28/05/1918
War Diary	Lhery Chatillon		28/05/1918	28/05/1918
War Diary	Chatillon Chambrecy		29/05/1918	29/05/1918
War Diary	Vendeuil Chatillon		29/05/1918	29/05/1918
War Diary	Lhery Chambrecy		29/05/1918	29/05/1918
War Diary	Chatillon Marieul Le Port		29/05/1918	29/05/1918
War Diary	Chambrecy Boujacourt		29/05/1918	29/05/1918
War Diary	Marieu Le Port Les Grande Fosse		30/05/1918	30/05/1918
War Diary	Boujacourt Nanteuil		29/05/1918	29/05/1918
War Diary	Marieul Le Port Igny-Le-Tard		29/05/1918	29/05/1918
War Diary	Les Grande Fosse Etang De Russon		31/05/1918	31/05/1918
War Diary	Bois De Boursalt Etang De Russon		31/05/1918	31/05/1918
War Diary	Etang De Russon		01/06/1918	01/06/1918
War Diary	Stang De Russon		01/06/1918	01/06/1918
War Diary	Le Mesnil		02/06/1918	03/06/1918
War Diary	Etg De Russon		04/06/1918	09/06/1918
War Diary	Connantre		10/06/1918	15/06/1918
War Diary	Allery		18/06/1918	23/06/1918
War Diary	Beauchamps		24/06/1918	18/07/1918
War Diary	Ligny-St. Flochel		18/07/1918	19/07/1918
War Diary	Bryas		19/07/1918	19/07/1918
War Diary	Beauchamps		20/07/1918	20/07/1918
War Diary	Ourton		20/07/1918	21/07/1918
War Diary	Barlin.		22/07/1918	22/07/1918
War Diary	Mt. St Eloy		22/07/1918	30/07/1918
Heading	War Diary August 1918. 8th D.A.C.			
War Diary	Mont St Eloi (Lens 2 I.)		01/08/1918	14/08/1918
War Diary	Mont St Eloi		16/08/1918	30/08/1918
War Diary	Mont St Eloi (Lens 2 I)		02/09/1918	15/09/1918
War Diary	Mont St Eloi		16/09/1918	03/10/1918
War Diary	Lens Map 1/100,000		04/10/1918	17/10/1918
War Diary	Valenciennes Map 1/100,000		18/10/1918	31/10/1918
War Diary	Antoing		01/12/1918	05/12/1918
War Diary	Tournai		06/12/1918	16/12/1918
War Diary	Leuze		17/12/1918	17/12/1918
War Diary	Bassilly		18/12/1918	31/12/1918
Operation(al) Order(s)	8th Divisional Artillery Order No. 96.		03/12/1918	03/12/1918

Operation(al) Order(s)	Amendment No. 1. To 8th Divisional Artillery Order No. 97.	14/12/1918	14/12/1918
Operation(al) Order(s)	8th. Divisional Artillery Order No. 97.	10/12/1918	10/12/1918
Miscellaneous	Table "A" Issued With 8th. D.A. Order No. 97, 10/12/18. "G" Day.		
War Diary	Bassilly	01/01/1919	31/04/1919
Heading	B.E.F. 8 Div. A.A. Section 1914 Sept To 1914 Dec.		
Heading	War Diary of the 1 Pr Anti Aircraft Detachment 8th Division From Date Of Formation To 30th November 1914		
War Diary	Hilsea	09/09/1914	19/10/1914
War Diary	Hursley	20/10/1914	04/11/1914
War Diary	Shampton-Le Harvre, Per SS Trattors Hall Le Harvre-Merville Per Rail	04/11/1914	04/11/1914
War Diary	Les Lauriers Near Merville	09/11/1914	13/11/1914
War Diary	Les Lauriers	13/11/1914	14/11/1914
War Diary	La Gorgue	14/11/1914	19/11/1914
War Diary	Le Drumez	20/11/1914	26/11/1914
War Diary	Rouge De Bout	27/11/1914	30/11/1914
Miscellaneous	Post Office Telegraphs.		
Miscellaneous	Post Office Telegraphs.	18/10/1914	18/10/1914
Miscellaneous	Post Office Telegraphs.		
Miscellaneous	4 pm Friday		
Miscellaneous	Post Office Telegraphs.		
Miscellaneous	To Confirm Telegram.		

1695

DIVISIONAL AMMUNITION COLUMN
NOV 1918 DIARY - NOT FOUND

8TH DIVISION

8TH DIVL AMMN COLUMN

NOV 1914 - MAY 1919

nil

A.2

121/2598

Ammunition Column
8th Division.

Vol I. 4 – 30.11.14

May 1919

Army Form C. 2118.

WAR DIARY
or
INTELLIGENCE SUMMARY.
(Erase heading not required.)

Instructions regarding War Diaries and Intelligence Summaries are contained in F. S. Regs., Part II. and the Staff Manual respectively. Title pages will be prepared in manuscript.

Hour, Date, Place			Summary of Events and Information	Remarks and references to Appendices
9.30pm	4 Nov/14	Hursley Camp	Marched from Camp to Southampton Docks (14 miles)	A/13
5.30am	5 Nov/14	Southampton	Embarked on S.S Archimedes	A/13
11.30pm	"	"	Left Southampton for Le Havre via The Needles	A/13
11.0am	6 Nov/14	Le Havre	Arrived Le Havre, Disembarkation complete 2 p.m.	A/13
10am	7 "	"	Arrived no 2 Rest Camp.	A/13
	11 Nov/14	Le Havre	Left Le Havre in 4 trains, H^3 Q^n 1 & 4 Secs to Strazeele, 2 & 3	A/13
	12 Nov/14		Secs to Merville	
	13 "	Merville	Billeted by sections in 3 farms & 1 chateau near Merville	A/13
	15 "	Estaires	Marched to Estaires (6 miles) and billeted by sections, took over duties of supplying Ammunition to Arty: Lahore Div^n at 3pm pending exchange of position of that Div^n with 8th Div^n	A/13
	18 "	"	Advanced Section of Ammunition Park under 2/Lt BEATTIE A.S.C attached to Am. Col^n and billeted in ESTAIRES	A/13
	24 "	"	Lt PATRICK 1 S/jt 2 B^m 1 SS 1 fitter 8 fjrs 16 Drs 1 Batman 3 Riding horses 16 heavy Draught horses & 13 Typ Carts were transferred to the RHA	A/13

(9 29 6) W 2794 100,000 8/14 H W V Forms/C. 2118/11.

Army Form C. 2118.

WAR DIARY
or
INTELLIGENCE SUMMARY.
(Erase heading not required.)

Instructions regarding War Diaries and Intelligence Summaries are contained in F.S. Regs., Part II. and the Staff Manual respectively. Title pages will be prepared in manuscript.

Hour, Date, Place	Summary of Events and Information	Remarks and references to Appendices
25th Nov 1914 ESTAIRES	6 the 3rd Cavalry Division to form part of the RHA Brigade Armn "Col" by that the 57th (How) Bty RFA was attached to 8th Division and its portion B Div.F.Am."Col" (1B" 16 men 2 horses & 4 G.S.Wagons) later joined 1m/Sec 8th Div RFA	MB
15th – 30th Nov "	During this period the following explosives etc were drawn for issue to R.E. & Infantry Brigades 1, Rifle Bombs 2. Hand Grenades 3. Very's Pistols and illum cartridges 4. Coloured Rockets 5. Very lights 6, gunpowder & electric detonators In addition the following were drawn for RA units for use in trenches 1. 18/pr High Explosive shell 2. 3 mortars and bombs for use in trenches.	MB

30-11-14.

Arthur Morris
Cap 8: Div Amm Colum.

121/3889

8th Div¹. Amm" Col"

Vol I. 1 - 31.12.14

WAR DIARY
or
INTELLIGENCE SUMMARY.
(Erase heading not required.)

Army Form C. 2118.

Hour, Date, Place	Summary of Events and Information	Remarks and references to Appendices
Estaires 1st to 31st Dec/14	During this period the 8th Divl: Amⁿ Colⁿ remained in Billets in ESTAIRES. Arthur Younger 8th Div^l A.C.	MW/B

8th, Division.

8thth, D. A. C.

January, 1915.

$\frac{121}{4210}$

8th Div'l Amm'n Col'n

Vol II. 10—28.1.15.

WAR DIARY or INTELLIGENCE SUMMARY

Army Form C. 2118.

(Erase heading not required.)

Instructions regarding War Diaries and Intelligence Summaries are contained in F.S. Regs., Part II. and the Staff Manual respectively. Title pages will be prepared in manuscript.

Hour, Date, Place	Summary of Events and Information	Remarks and references to Appendices
Estaires 10 Jan/15	A draft of 8 R.F.A gunners arrived from Le Havre	
" 11 Jan/15	A draft of 8 R.G.A gunners arrived from Le Havre	
" 12 Jan/15	Regtl Sergt Major H.T. Collison left for Base on promotion to Lieut (Gaz'd Commission 4 Jan)	
" 17 Jan/15	Lieut J.M Muyne posted to 33rd Bty R.F.A	
" 27 Jan/15	A detachment consisting of 1 Offr, 1 BSM, 17 men, 25 horses & 4 G.S. wagons were attached to the Column, this detachment was the portion of Div'l Amm Col" which joined the 8th Div" with the 5B (4.5 How) Bty R.F.A.	
" 28 Jan/15	A detachment consisting of 1 Sgt, 1 Cpl, 1 B's, 2 gs's, 1 S.S. & 16 frs & Drs 24 horses 6 G.S. wagons were attached to the Column, this detachment was the portion of the Div'l Am" Col" which joined (from) the 8th Div" with the 109th (4.7 Heavy) Bty R.G.A from Lahore Div"	

J.M.M. Moran
G.8.D.A.C.

8th, Division.

8th, D. A. C.

February, 1915.

A.2

121/4468

8ten Div.l Amm.n Col.n

Vol III 1 - 28.2.15

Army Form C. 2118.

WAR DIARY
or
INTELLIGENCE SUMMARY.
(Erase heading not required.)

Instructions regarding War Diaries and Intelligence Summaries are contained in F.S. Regs., Part II. and the Staff Manual respectively. Title pages will be prepared in manuscript.

Hour, Date, Place	Summary of Events and Information	Remarks and references to Appendices
Estaires 1st Feb 1915	2nd Lieut R.W. Gate R.F.A. (Sp. Res.) joined from Base (Havre) and was posted to no 1 Section	PWB
Estaires 2nd Feb. 1915	2nd Lieut G.L.R. Wisely posted to 59th Battery R.F.A. and left the Did A.m. Col.	PWB
" "	2nd Lieuts E.H. Wenham & F.H. Allan joined the Column from Base and were posted to no 3 Section	PWB
3rd " 3rd to 5th Feb 1915	Owing to the closing of many of the roads to heavy motor traffic during this period Am. had to be conveyed from HAZEBROUCK by the Column in addition about 30 tons of R.E. stores were conveyed from R.E. Parks at STAZEELE to 15th Co. R.E. at NOUVEAU MONDE on the 4th Feb.	PWB
" 7th Feb.	The Section 1 Did A.m. Col. accompanying the 53rd (How.) Bty, R.F.A. B/Ho t Div - strength 1 Cpl. 1 W.O. 17 men, 25 horses & 4 G.S. Wagons Detachment from no 4 Sec 1st Div.l Am. Col. accompanying 40 (How) Bty R.F.A. joined 8th Div.l Am.l Col and was attached to no 3 Sec near EPINETTE - strength 1 Sgt. 1 W.O. 16 men, 24 horses & 5 G.S. Wagons	PWB

Army Form C. 2118.

WAR DIARY
or
INTELLIGENCE SUMMARY.
(Erase heading not required.)

Instructions regarding War Diaries and Intelligence Summaries are contained in F.S. Regs., Part II. and the Staff Manual respectively. Title pages will be prepared in manuscript.

Hour, Date, Place	Summary of Events and Information	Remarks and references to Appendices
Estaires 17th Feb 1915	The Section of the Dist Am Col accompanying the 58th (How) Bty RFA left the Div - strength 1 Sgt 1 Bdr, 16 men, 24 horses & 5 G.S. Wagons	P.M.B.
" 21st Feb 1915	The Section of Dist Am Col accompanying the 40th Heavy Battery RGA (4.7") left the Div - strength 1 Officer (2Lt Weir) 3 NCOs 19 men 24 horses 6 G.S. Wagons & 1 motor cycle	P.M.B.
" 23rd Feb 1915	The Section of Dist Am Col accompanying the 57th (How) Bty RFA left the 8th Div - strength 1 Bdr 16 men 27 horses & 4 G.S. Wagons	P.M.B.
" 28th Feb 1915	Lt-Col F.A. Elton left the Column on posting to 25th Brigade R.F.A. (1st Div)	P.M.B.

J.H. Flynn Lt-Col RFA
Comdg 8th Dist Am Col

WAR DIARY
or
INTELLIGENCE SUMMARY

(Erase heading not required.)

Army Form C. 2118.

Hour, Date, Place	Summary of Events and Information	Remarks and references to Appendices
Feb 25th 1915	Company reviewed in front ST OMER	
Feb 26th 1915	Company marched on parade ST OMER	
Feb 27th 1915	1 Bus inspected at 10.30 am	
	6 late orders from CATEORNE D M & BEGT	
	5 N Q 2 = Corps	
	1 Busses are posted at 9.0am	
	to late Madame Guerin downs & Hove	
	Corps H.Q.	
Feb 28th 1915	1 Bus (P H.Q) CAV Corps CHATEAU AN IMETTE	
	1 Bus (e) 1st Indian Corps ST VENANT	
	1 Bus (e) the 1st Corps CHOQUES S.	
	1 Bus (e) the 2nd Corps BAILLEUL	
	1 Bus (e) the 3rd Corps BRIELEUL	
	1 Bus (e) 11th 3rd Corp. MERVILLE	
	1 Bus (e) 11th ST Corp.	

8th, Division.

8th, D. A. C.

March, 1915.

121/4779

8th Div. l'Armée "Col"

Vol IV 1-29.3.15

WAR DIARY
or
INTELLIGENCE SUMMARY

Army Form C. 2118.

Hour, Date, Place	Summary of Events and Information	Remarks and references to Appendices
Merville 1st March 1915	The Am" Col" moved from Estaires the four sections being billeted at LE TOUQUET just N of HAVRESKERQUE the Headquarters being at COURT COURTEFROIE Farm 1½ miles NW of MERVILLE	
" 2nd March 1915	A small section under Lt HEDLEY was established at LA GORGUE to deal with bombs grenades and other explosives used by the Infantry. This section issued these stores direct to 2nd Brigade S.A.A Reserves and not through RA Brigade Am" Cols.	
" 3rd " "	The Column ceased issuing Ammunition to Brigade Am" Col" and the following system was instituted. The Am" Park from HAVERSKERQUE established a Dump advanced Sec" on the Merville – Hazebrouck Road 1 m. L N of Merville. The H.Q" & "Div" Am" Col" were connected by telephone to the IV Corps Signal Office Exchange in Merville. An orderly from each Brigade was attached to H.Q" & DAC. By these means	

WAR DIARY
or
INTELLIGENCE SUMMARY.
(Erase heading not required.)

Army Form C. 2118.

Instructions regarding War Diaries and Intelligence Summaries are contained in F.S. Regs., Part II. and the Staff Manual respectively. Title pages will be prepared in manuscript.

Hour, Date, Place	Summary of Events and Information	Remarks and references to Appendices
Merville 6th Mar 1915	Demand for Am" could be made by telephone direct to H²Qrs DAC whence an orderly could be sent to Brigade Am" Col's telling them to issue the Am" required, calling at the Advanced Sec" of Park on his way to warn them of the demand. The Brigade Am" Cols then sent up the Am" required and refilled at the Park on the way back. Lt-Col & Brevet Col F.W. Boteler R.F.A joined the Col" an" assumed command.	PAB PAB
13th May 1915	Nos 1, 2 & 3 Sections moved to Billets East of MERVILLE between LA BRIANNE and the river LYS and resumed the supply of Am" to Brigade Am" Cols. The Advanced Sec" of Am" Park returned to HAVERSKERQUE. Owing to the bad and narrow roads the Am" Park was unable to send Lorries up to the Div Am Col so carts were filled at a Refilling Point on the MERVILLE - BETHUNE Road. A motor cyclist from 7th Am" Park was attached to H²Qrs D.A.C. for intercommunication	PAB

WAR DIARY
or
INTELLIGENCE SUMMARY

(Erase heading not required.)

Army Form C. 2118.

Hour, Date, Place	Summary of Events and Information	Remarks and references to Appendices
Merville 9th Mar/15	15 men were attached to 5th RHA Brigade for duty with Trench Mortars	
13th Mar "	6 men were sent to 5th RHA Brigade to replace casualties with Mortar Party	
23rd Mar "	All sections were concentrated near COURTEFROIE F{m}	
27th Mar "	The 8th Div moved to SAILLY, the Div A.M. remaining near MERVILLE, the Bomb Section however moved to near SAILLY	
4th Mar [sic]	R-S-M (W.O.) S.S. Goodall joined the Col. on promotion	
10 Mar	Lieut E.G. Stead was admitted to hospital	
25th Mar	Capt L.B. Rich left the Column on posting to 1st Sqdy RHA	
31st Mar	Capt M.H. Magrath joined the Column vice Capt Rich from 2nd Div.	
" "		
25th Mar [sic]	8 G S wagons complete with drivers & horses with all the 4.7 Am were sent to 8th Heavy Brigade Am Col. on reorganisation 8 Am Col. for Heavy Artillery	
29 Mar	The 6 wagons with 4.5 Am from 4th Div supplying 27th Brigade were transferred to 7th Div A Col.	

M.H.Arthur Lt.Col. 1st Col RFA
Com{g} 8th Div A.Am Col.

8th, Division.

8th, D. A. C.

April, 1915.

12.1/5/08

8th Divisional Ammn Col"

Vol V 5 — 28.4.15

AV
R6

Army Form C. 2118.

WAR DIARY or INTELLIGENCE SUMMARY.

(Erase heading not required.)

8th Divl Ammn Coln

Hour, Date, Place	Summary of Events and Information	Remarks and references to Appendices
Merville 5th April 1915 9th April	Lt O.J. Jones left the Column on posting to Trench Mortar Sec. The Column moved to billets N. of the LYS between ESTAIRES and SAILLY	19-4-15 Arthy. 2407A. II Corps dated
Estaires 19th April	Major C. H. Burdon (Adjutant) left the column on posting to 27th Division (133rd Battery) Capt. L. Sherlock appointed A/Adj.	
21st April	The 4.5" How: Section of the 7th Div: Amn Col came down attached to No 1 Sec. 8th Divn Amn Col. Strength 1 Subaltn 1 Bn. 29 men + 29 horses.	
24.5 "	2 G.S. wagons (6 men + 12 horses) belonging to 4.5 How: Sec: left to rejoin the 7th D.A.C.	
26 "	2 G.S. wagons (4 drivers, 4 gunners, 8 horses) left to rejoin 7th D.A.C.	
27 "	Six Heavy wagons arrived (12 horses, 1 Cpl (A.S.C.) + 6 men) came to complete est: for 4.5 How: Sect. & were attached to No 1 Sec. a/c D.A.C.	

Army Form C. 2118.

WAR DIARY
or
INTELLIGENCE SUMMARY.
(Erase heading not required.)

Instructions regarding War Diaries and Intelligence Summaries are contained in F.S. Regs., Part II. and the Staff Manual respectively. Title pages will be prepared in manuscript.

Hour, Date, Place	Summary of Events and Information	Remarks and references to Appendices
ESTAIRES 27 April	4 wagons, 1 Cpl. 17 Drivers + 2 gunners, left No1 Sect. to join 7 Bt A.C. They belong to 37th 6 Bns. 4.3" how.	
28 "	No 1 Sec. 7th Div. Am. Col. (consisting of 2 off., 106 other ranks 77 L.D. horses, 38 H.D. horses + 29 wagons) seem to be attached to 6 Bn D.A.C.	
28/29 "	Working party 10 y. 1 N.C.O. + 30 men went to trenches to dig for trench mortars. 6 Dr. Wallace + Dr. Cresswell returns. 1 by wounded.	

1-5-15

M Schuster Jones
O>8 S/8 Ac

8th, Division.

8th, D. A. C.

May, 1915.

12/54-81

Army Form C. 2118.

WAR DIARY
or
INTELLIGENCE SUMMARY. 8th Div. Am. Col.
(Erase heading not required.)

Instructions regarding War Diaries and Intelligence Summaries are contained in F.S. Regs., Part II. and the Staff Manual respectively. Title pages will be prepared in manuscript.

Hour, Date, Place	Summary of Events and Information	Remarks and references to Appendices
ESTAIRES May 4th 1915	The 8th Divl. Am. Col. moved into new billets in and around DOULIEU #11	
" 5th	No.1 Sec. 7th D.A.C. consisting of 2 Off., 109 other ranks, 11 riders, 84 L.D. horses + 36 H.D. horses, left at 9 am for the 7th D.A.C.	
" 6th	The 4.5 How. Sec. 7th D.A.C., consisting of 43 N.C.O.s & men, 48 L.D. horses, 8 G.S. wagons, joined + was attached to 8th D.A.C.	
" 6th, 7th + 8th	The 8th D.A.C. distributed about 76 tons of ammunition for the impending operation.	
" 9th	The 8th D.A.C. moved to its former billets in vacated TROU BAYARD at 4 am. The column supplied 4,123 rds. am. R.H. & R.F.A. for the battle.	
" 10th	Capt. U. M. Myrath R.F.A. + Lt. T.H Alland R.F.A. left the Column. 2nd Lieut to join the 33rd Bdm., R.F.A.	

(9 29 6) W 2794 100,000 8/14 H W V Forms/C. 2118/11.

WAR DIARY or INTELLIGENCE SUMMARY.

Army Form C. 2118.

II

(Erase heading not required.)

Hour, Date, Place	Summary of Events and Information	Remarks and references to Appendices
N.q. ESTAIRES.		
May 10th 1915 9.10	Capt. M. Magrath to join the 3rd Batt. Lt. G.H. Huxley (Bomb Section, detached from 8th D.A.C.) engaged in carrying bombs, grenades etc up to firing line under heavy shell fire.	
" 10	Two thirds of 4.5 How. Section A (consisting of 41 N.C.Os & men & 46 horses) left the 8th D.A.C. to join the Y & Z D.A.C. on the SOUTHERN, ESTAIRES - SAILLY 5 ROAD.	
" 11	Col. F.M. S. Peake returned to 8th D.A.C. from Hqs 8th Div having preceded there on 9th inst. for the purpose of assisting in distributing of ammunition during the fight on 9th & 10th.	
" 9th to 12th inc.	The farm at present occupied by Hqs. 8th Div. Am. Col. (called End de Bac Ferme) was used by the German Crown Prince about last October (1914). The Germans behaved very kindly to the occupants, took anything	

WAR DIARY or INTELLIGENCE SUMMARY

Army Form C. 2118.

Hour, Date, Place	Summary of Events and Information	Remarks and references to Appendices
N. of ESTAIRES. MAY 9-12	Vet. was unkind to them, & turned the Baron, who is about 80 years of age, out of his bed to make room for one of the staff officers.	
" 13th	Capt. L. J. Mitchell R.F.A. (ex-adv. of the 8th D.A.C.) for duty. He came from England.	
" 15th	1/2 Lt. H.P.W. Musgrave & 2/Lt. H.C. Tenney (from 45th & 65th A.C.) joined the 5th D.A.C. for duty. 2/Lt. Musgrave from 1st Batt. O.T.C.	
" 16th	2/Lt. E.H. Wenham left the Column on being posted to the 3rd Batt. O.T.C.	13-6-'15
" 15th	Capt. C. Sherlock appointed Adj. 5th D.A.C.	Arty. 4 Corps 2915 A
" 17th	1 Offr. & 13 men returned for duty to the column from the trench mortars.	
" 19th	Capt. H.L. Gillespie (from 33rd Bri. Am. Col.) joined the 8th D.A.C. for duty (No 3 Sec.)	
" 21st/22nd	2/Lt. W. Musgrave & 2/Lt. McCallum proceeded to 5th & 63rd H.B. & 33rd 63rd F.A. Bm. respectively to learn	

Army Form C. 2118.

WAR DIARY
or
INTELLIGENCE SUMMARY.

(Erase heading not required.)

Instructions regarding War Diaries and Intelligence Summaries are contained in F.S. Regs., Part II. and the Staff Manual respectively. Title pages will be prepared in manuscript.

Hour, Date, Place	Summary of Events and Information	Remarks and references to Appendices
N. of ESTAIRES. May 21+22	Observation duties.	
" 22	Capt. H.J. Gillespie left the Column to take command of 33rd Divl. Am. Col. was Capt. Paul	
" 25th	2/Lt. H.P. Wyndham Musgrave left the Column for England, to report to War Office in writing. G.R.T.D.(S.R.)	
" 26th	2/Lt. S.J.K. Collins & 2/Lt. L.J. Teeling joined the 8th D.A.C. from the base	
" 31st	2/Lt. J.R. McCallum left the Column on posting to 55th O.Batt. G.R.F.A. (Hon.) with effect from 30th May.	

J M Sutton John
Lt R.F.A.

8th, Division.

8th, D. A. C.

June, 1915.

8ᵗʰ Division

8ᵗʰ Divis: Arras u Col

Vol VII 5. — 28.6.15

WAR DIARY
or
INTELLIGENCE SUMMARY.

(Erase heading not required.)

Army Form C. 2118.

8th Div. Amm. Col.

Hour, Date, Place	Summary of Events and Information	Remarks and references to Appendices
1915		
N. of ESTAIRES June 5th	2/Lt. H.E. Well joined the Column from England.	
" 6th	The column was issued with Anti-Gas Respirators. All ranks that could be spared helped to a lecture on the use of Respirators.	
" 8th	The guns of the 5th R.H.A. Bri. were changed to 18 pr. This necessitated changing 13 pr wheel no. The carried to 18 pr am. which were done today. Owing to its increase in size could not carry the full establishment of 18 pr Amm. Transport (4 top cards or 2 G.S. wagons) to carry full set intended for a working party went to trenches to dig. Party esc-orted of Lt. Studward & 16 men. One man (gr. Bennett No 2 Sec.) very slightly wounded.	
" 13th	Cpl. H. Bruckshaw (late 7, 3rd Batt. 6, 7, 4) & now attached to this column was awarded the D.C.M. for gallant con-duct in mending his telephone wire under heavy fire at	

WAR DIARY or INTELLIGENCE SUMMARY

Army Form C. 2118.

(Erase heading not required.)

Instructions regarding War Diaries and Intelligence Summaries are contained in F. S. Regs., Part II. and the Staff Manual respectively. Title pages will be prepared in manuscript.

Hour, Date, Place		Summary of Events and Information	Remarks and references to Appendices
1916.			
N. d'ESTAIRES	June 13th	NEUVE CHAPELLE. The distribution was made by Major General Davies.	
"	14	2/Lt H.C.Terry left the Column on posting to 45th Bm. O.T.F.S. 2/Lt. F.H. Wenham rejoined the Column from the 45th Bm. O.T.F.S.	
"	17	The R.E. wagon containing the explosives (reserve) hitherto attached to the 6th Lee. kingform to 62nd Section.	
"	23rd	One-third return. T.S.7 & F.Coll. (4.6) 43rd Bri. Div. Am. Col. joined the Column from Lenth of Div. The 3 Lee enrolled of 181.D. horses, 7 mules, 19 N.C.O. drivers, 4 wagons, 204 rds Lyddite + 10 rds shrapnel.	
"	24	Lt. G. H. Hadley left for England on 7 days leave.	
"	24	2/Lt D.H.Lack rejoined the Column as Interpreter, with effect from today. Routine order 6th Div. 565. 24-6-15; now W/Br. a/w. Gunner transferred to A.S.C. with effect from 5th June.	

WAR DIARY or INTELLIGENCE SUMMARY.

Army Form C. 2118.

(Erase heading not required.)

Hour, Date, Place	Summary of Events and Information	Remarks and references to Appendices
N. FESTUBERT Jun 25	Col. F.W. Batlelle proceeded to ENGLAND on 7 days leave	
" 26	2/Lt-A.O.T. Gamme joined 8th Div. Train.	28-6-15
" 28	2/Lt. D.H. Lock posted to & joined the 8th D.A.C.	8th Div. Gen. Order 684

J.B. Musprove(?) Major R.F.A.
for Col.
Comdg. 8th Div. Am. Col.

8th, Division.

8th, D. A. C.

July, 1915.

137/6231

8th Division.

8th Div: Ammn Colⁿ
Vet <u>xxx</u>
1 – 30-7 – 15

WAR DIARY or INTELLIGENCE SUMMARY. 8th Div. Am. Col.

Army Form C. 2118.

Hour, Date, Place	Summary of Events and Information	Remarks and references to Appendices
1915		
N. of ESTAIRES. July 1st	Nine bycycles, one mallese cart & 10 horses received from 8 Div. train. (Below transport for extra Amm. to be carried in Lt Column.) 6 to No 1, 26 to 2, 26 to No 3 Section	
" 2nd	2/Lt H. Eaton O2.F.A. joined the Column from the base, formerly with A Batt.	
" 6th	2/Lt C. Atwell O2.F.A. joined the Column from the base	
" 7th	2/Lt L. J. Tebby O2.F.A. posted to 3rd R.H. & A. Bar.	
" 10th	2/Lt Dimy Carter O2.F.A. joined the Column from the base	
" 11th	2/Lt L. J. K. Collins posted to 3rd R.H.A. Bar.	
" 13th	Major L. Mortimer R.F.A. from No 1 Lt. 8th D.A.C. posted to 3 2nd Batt. O2.F.A.	
" 14th	Capt. G. L. Fagan O2.F.A. joined the Col. from the Base	
" 19th	Capt. L.E. Fagan O2.F.A. joined the Col. from the base	
" 21st	2/Lt W.F. Anderson O2.F.A. joined the Col. from the base	
" 26th	2/Lt H.E. Webb to England	
" 29th	Capt. R.A. Lloyd O3.Gunnery O2.F.A. joined Col. from Base	
" 30th	Capt G. L. Fagan left Column for 7th Division	III Corps 7/4609/39. 23-7-15.

Army Form C. 2118.

WAR DIARY
or
INTELLIGENCE SUMMARY.

(Erase heading not required.)

Instructions regarding War Diaries and Intelligence Summaries are contained in F. S. Regs., Part II. and the Staff Manual respectively. Title pages will be prepared in manuscript.

Hour, Date, Place	Summary of Events and Information	Remarks and references to Appendices
N. of ESTAIRES July 30th	Capt. G. L. Barredaile R.F.A. joined the column from the base.	

E Sherlock Capt
Adj. 8th Div. Am. Col.
1-8-15

8th, Division.

8th, D. A. C.

August, 1915.

8th Division

6598/121

8th Divl: Animn Colln
Vol IX
from 2 to 31. 8. 15

WAR DIARY or INTELLIGENCE SUMMARY.

8th Divl. Am. Col.

Army Form C. 2118.

Hour, Date, Place	Summary of Events and Information	Remarks and references to Appendices
1915		
N. of ESTAIRES. Aug 2nd	Lt. E.G. Redmond attached to 57th Batt. R.F.A. with effect from 2nd August.	
"	Lt. D'A.O. Carden attached to 45th Bri. with effect from 1st August.	
" 5th	Major L. Thurlow rejoined the Column from 32nd Batt. R.F.A.	
" 6th	Lt. E.H. Wenham left the Column — being attached to 45th Bri. Am. Col.	
" 8th	Lt. C.G. Omelthon, Reserve R.F.A. joined the Column, having been for some months an civil prisoner.	
" 12th	Lt. D.H. Zoch left the Column on posting to 4th Corps H.Qrs.	
" 12th	Lt. F.W. Tabutt, Lt. O.E.P. Balter, Lt. B.H. Fry joined the Column from Base.	
" 14th	Lt. W.F. Anterton posted to 33rd Bri. Am. Col.	
" 14th	Lt. F.W. Tabutt posted to 45th Bri. Am. Col.	
" 14th	8th Divisional Horse Show held on bank of River Lys.	
" 2nd	1 Section 2nd D.A.C. arrived trans attached to 8th D.A.C. They consist of 1/45 all ranks, 10 horses, 186 mules, 30 wagons.	

Army Form C. 2118.

WAR DIARY
or
INTELLIGENCE SUMMARY.
(Erase heading not required.)

Instructions regarding War Diaries and Intelligence Summaries are contained in F.S. Regs., Part II. and the Staff Manual respectively. Title pages will be prepared in manuscript.

Hour, Date, Place	Summary of Events and Information	Remarks and references to Appendices
1915		
N.J ESTAIRES. Aug 18th	Capt. C. A. E. Cahill R.F.A. joined the column from 47th Divn.	
" "	Maj. Gen. H. Hudson, accompanied by Brig. Gen. Nickalson in-	
" "	spected the Column. The General congratulated the column on parade.	
" 20	2nd Lt. C. Stuart left the Column on posting to 5, 7, & 8 Batt. 62. F. A. (4.5 How.)	
" 21st	Capt. C. A. E. Cahill posted to 33rd Bn. R.F.A. with effect from 11-6-15	
" 22nd	2/Lt. B. H. Fry to be attached to 45th Bn. R.F.A. with effect from 21-8-15	
" 22nd	2/Lt. O. E. S. Butler posted as Orderly Officer to 128 Bn R.F.A. " " 2-8-15	
" 23rd	2/Lt. R. Ross joined the Column the base.	
" 24th	R.S.M. J. Fordell (G.F.) promoted to Commissioned Rank with effect from 19-8-15 (Arthy. 3rd Corps were A/6112, 23-8-15)	
" 24	Capt. G. L. Barrowdale posted to 54 R.H.A. Am. Col. with effect from 21st Aug.	
" 28	2nd Lt. R. Ross attached to 128 Bn. R.F.A. with effect from 27-8-15	
" 16 31	The Column performed numerous fatigues, including 36 men daily for Hly. dug-outs.	
" 31	The Brass Band revived in the Column, started playing in afternoon at No 5 Stab.	

F.M. Sletter Colonel

8th, Division.

8th, D. A. C.

September, 1915.

121/699

8th Bivouac

8th Div: Amm n Col n
Col x
Sept. 15

Army Form C. 2118.

WAR DIARY
or
INTELLIGENCE SUMMARY.

I   8th Divn. Am. Col.

(Erase heading not required.)

Hour, Date, Place	Summary of Events and Information	Remarks and references to Appendices
DOULIEU Sept. 2nd/15	The Column moved to billets in & around DOULIEU.	
" 8 "	2/Lt. H.F. Jupp joined the Column from the Base.	
" 8 "	2/Lt. J.E. Humberstone posted to Column, but attached to 45th Bn. R.F.A., to which unit he went.	
" 10 "	2/Lt. C. Sheat rejoined the Column from 57th Batt. vice 2/Lt. H.E. Jupp who left the Column on posting to 57th Batt.	
" 13 "	The 4th Section (4.5") ceased to exist as such from today. Arty. 1st Army 1405/32A Anti. 8th Divn. It was primarily attached posted to as a complete sub-section dated 6-9-15 to No.1 Section. This was done as No.1 Section has for 3rd Corps G/522 7/15 some months one sub-section short of full establish- 8th Divn. 1562/9 ment, + no matter how the 4.5 section was dis- posed of, now the 3 Sections could be supplied in men + horses from the Column.	
" 16 "	2/Lt. R. Skelton RFA joined the Column from the Base	

Army Form C. 2118.

WAR DIARY
or
INTELLIGENCE SUMMARY. 8th Div. Am. Col.

(Erase heading not required.)

Hour, Date, Place	Summary of Events and Information	Remarks and references to Appendices
DOULIEU Sept 17th 1915	Capt. T. J. Mitchie R.F.A. left the Column for England on posting to Home Establishment.	
" 17th	2/Lt. R.N. Wallis R.F.A. joined the Column from the Base.	
" 17th	No.1 Eastern Canadian Divn. Am. Col. consisting of 2 Offs.	
" 10.9	Other ranks 137 horses, 21 G.S. wagons, 206 Sm.	
"	18 pr. dumped arrived in billets near Doulieu & was pr. attached to this Column.	
" 19th	2/Lt. R. McLellin attached to 33rd Bror. R.F.A. left the Column.	
" 19th	The supply of Ammunition for forthcoming operations are on a new principle, which is :- In allotment of 180 rds per 18 pr. Gun (70 Shrapnel & 30 H.E.) & 60 rds per 4.5" gun was dumped at 8th Div. Amn. Col. In addition to this, a whole unit of amn establishment was dumped	

Army Form C. 2118.

WAR DIARY or INTELLIGENCE SUMMARY.

8th Divl. Amn. Col.

(Erase heading not required.)

Hour, Date, Place	Summary of Events and Information	Remarks and references to Appendices
DOULIEU Sept 1914 1915		
20th	at 8th D.A.C. The 2nd Ech. Est. consists of 75 rds per 18 pr gun, 40 rds per 4.5 gun & 920 rds S.A.A. The principle to be adopted is that the whole of the allotment dumps is to be used first after which no ammunition is issued, gun wagons will fill up from 6nd dumps which will be replaced from amm. in proper 2nd Ech. Carts. The 23rd Divn. have attached to 8th D.A.C. a complete (18 pr & 4.5 gun) Section.	
21.9.15	The 8th D.A.C. + attached sections sent to Bri. Amn. Cols. many thousands of rounds from special dumps.	
22	2Lt. A.E.W. Rogers joined the Column from the Base.	Auth, R.A. Lebon 3rd Echelon
22	R.S.M., A.E. Crofton joined the Column on promotion from 18th L Bde B.C., F.A., 7th Divn.	R.A. 11193 A/17/5
23rd	2/Lt. Henderson Clarke left the Column for duty with Kite-Balloon Section, 7th Wing R.F.C., AIRE.	Auth, 3rd Corps No A/87, 18-9-15

Army Form C. 2118.

WAR DIARY
or
INTELLIGENCE SUMMARY.   8th Divl. Am. Col.

(Erase heading not required.)

Instructions regarding War Diaries and Intelligence Summaries are contained in F. S. Regs., Part II. and the Staff Manual respectively. Title pages will be prepared in manuscript.

Hour, Date, Place	Summary of Events and Information	Remarks and references to Appendices
1915		
DOULIEU Sept 23rd	The 8th D.A.C. attached hitherto continued to supply large quantities of Amn. from advanced Park Dump.	
" 24	2 men of the distance from Bn. Am. Col. (about 4 miles) & men of equivalent in the mornw, the 8th D.A.C. & 2 of attached batteries moved about 2 miles nearer Sailly. This necessitated shifting the Park Dump, but because of instructions which in expeditious manner. it could not be carried out until early morning on 25th when instructions ceased.	
N. of SAILLY 25	The whole of the Park establishment (containing 1) 7,200 18 Ibr, 14,40 4.5 & 9,2000 5AA.) was dumped at a new refilling point in about 2 hours.	
" 25	2/Lt H.W. Bromley posted to 8th D.A.C. (from 33rd Bn. Am. Col.) vice 2/Lt R. Walker posted to 33rd R.F.A. Bde.	
" 24	2/Lt R. Shelton posted to 33rd R.F.A. Bn.	

WAR DIARY or INTELLIGENCE SUMMARY

Army Form C. 2118.

8th Divn. Ammn. Col.

Hour, Date, Place	Summary of Events and Information	Remarks and references to Appendices
N.J. SAILLY Sept 25/15	The 8th D.A.C. Collected actions supplied enormous quantities of Ammn. 20000 rds 18 pr Shrapnel, over 12000 14 pr H.E., over 2000 4.5" Ammn. The guns of 8th Divn. & 3 attached Brigades fired 197 4.6 in Shrapnel, 2764 4.5" H.E., 2046 18 pr H.E. & 19131 18 pr Shrapnel, above figures refer to 18 pr & 4.5" guns only. Owing to Divn. Ammn. Columns demanding more than their establishment the greatest difficulty was experienced in maintaining the supply of 18 pr shrapnel (A) & 4.5 Lyddite (Bx). The Divl. Cart. having formed 40 mules to obtain them. Bx could be obtained by Divl. Cash, all rostreds (III Corps & Indian) having run out of it. No 3 Section 2nd D.A.C. rejoined the 20th Div.	25th G.O.C. wrote to hand of 26th Bde. See Nicholson O.R.D.D. was not to properly handle the column for the work carried out on 25th. 22nd M.I. Bn. also mentioned the 4 work carried down to Colonel –– 23rd Divn.
26 4/15	Half of 18 pr Sec. Composite Sec. 23rd Divn. rejoined the 23rd Divn.	

Army Form C. 2118.

WAR DIARY
or
INTELLIGENCE SUMMARY.   8th Div. Am. Col.

(Erase heading not required.)

Hour, Date, Place		Summary of Events and Information	Remarks and references to Appendices

N.of SAILLY Apl 26th 1915.

As one Batt. (5th), 45th Bri. R.F.A. was attached to 25th Div., ⅓ portion of 18 pr. Sec, No 2 Lie., No 2 S.A.C. was attached to 25th Div. (31 all ranks, 22 horses, 13 bp - carts + 1 G.S. wagon, the whole in charge of 2 Lt- Rogers).

27th No 2 Section Am. S.A.C. rejoined the Eschelon S.A.C.

24th Ammn Section 23rd S.A.C. rejoined the 23rd S.A.C.

29th 2/Lt. Brinsley admitted to Convalescent home

30th The 8th S.A.C. moved into its former billets in and agound DOULIEU.

The tetron ammn in charge of Park Dump.

30th The ⅓ portion of No 2 Section 18 pr Section rejoined the 2nd Section 8th S.A.C.

4 pm 2/Lt. T.C. Baynes R.F.A + 2/Lt T. Goodman R.F.A joined the Column from the Base.

DOULIEU

A.M. Shetu ? Maud
T. (can) 8th D.A.C.

8th, Division.

8t h, D. A. C.

October, 1915.

121/7368

8th Kiwain

8th Dist. inina " Col.
Vol XL
Oct 15

WAR DIARY
or
INTELLIGENCE SUMMARY.   8th Divl. Am. Col
(Erase heading not required.)

Army Form C. 2118.

Hour, Date, Place	Summary of Events and Information	Remarks and references to Appendices
DOULIEU Oct 2nd 1915		
2nd	2/Lt N F Brown & 2/Lt H B Taylor joined the column from the Base	
	2/Lt E A W Regan attached to 5th Bn. D.A.C.	
	2/Lt T C Rayner " " 33rd " D.A.C.	
	2/Lt T Goodman " " 45th " "	
	Brigadier Carpenter Inspected & passed the column	
3	Sgt H B Taylor posted to 1st Bn the column as F.S.I. man	
3	2nd/Lt L Lee posted to column from 12.9 2d Bn. D.T.S.	
4	Lt R A Pellman joined the column from the Base	
5	2/Lt J H Hamilton " " " " " "	
5	Lt R A Palmer posted to 45th Bn. D.T.S.	
10	2/Lt C A G Nicholson posted to S.R. & D.A.C. (3 Division)	
	attached to Hdqr A.S.C. 8th Div.	
13	Lt A Butler joined the column from 18 "Ash" Aux. suppr (4.5 Res)	
13	2/Lt O J Freedman " " to Base was medically unfit 2nd Bn A.S.C.	
13	2/Lt J A D Ross joined the column from the Base (4.5 Res.)	

WAR DIARY
or
INTELLIGENCE SUMMARY.

Army Form C. 2118.

8th Div. Ammn. Col.

(Erase heading not required.)

Hour, Date, Place	Summary of Events and Information	Remarks and references to Appendices
DOWIEIA Oct 14.4.15	2nd Lt J H Handcock posted to B.A.C. & B.A.C.	
14	2nd Lt A Butler & 2nd Lt A Cross posted to 33rd Bm & 6th Bm Q.F.A.Q. R.H.A respectively	
17	Three dumps of Ammunition were established see Adly. Ft O No 9852 17.10.15	
	Col amm Shrapnel back to Kantara.	
24	Lt A Butler returned to Column	
26	Lt H Querripel & 2nd Lt A R Welby joined the Column from the Base, & posted to B 3rd Echelon respectively	Coll Temp commanders
30	Lt R McLean Hunter joined the column from the Base & posted to No 3 Section	
1.16.15	In addition to supplying ammunition to Column furnished numerous fatigues & working parties.	

8th, Division.

8th, D. A. C.

November, 1915.

8th Division

8th Divl Ammn Col

Nov.

Vol XII

121/755

WAR DIARY
INTELLIGENCE SUMMARY. 8th Div. Amm. Col.

Army Form C. 2118.

Hour, Date, Place		Summary of Events and Information	Remarks and references to Appendices
DOULIEU	Nov 1915 1st	Capt. L.E. Fagan & Lt. H. Quarry posted to 33rd Bde. Amm. Col. & 126th Bde. R.F.A. respectively.	
"	3rd	2/Lt. J.H.D. Orrs & 2/Lt. E.R.W. Orgen posted to 5th F. Bde. Ft. H.A. from 1-11-15.	
"	6th	2/Lt. N.T. Bacon sent to 5th Bde. R.H.A.	
"	1st	2/Lt. R.V. Wallis posted to 33rd Bde. R.F.A.	
"	22nd	2/Lt G.S. Barrows RFA joined from base	
"	28th	Capt E Sherlock – attached 55th Bty RFA	
"	"	2/Lt e.G.G. Nicholson – " – 2 " RFA	
"	"	2/Lt G.S. Barrows " – 45th Bde RFA	
"	27th	2/Lt H Eaton – appointed A/Adjutant 8th DAC	effect from 24th Nov
"	"	2/Lt H. Hogan Gaul, T.D. Weldon, H.C. Harris, K.W. Gilbert,	
"	"	C.B. Golding, Wallace, A. Bell all special Reserve joined	
"	"	from base.	
"	"	Lieut A.D. Butler to England.	
"	29th	2/Lieut F.L. Lee attached 33rd Bde, 2/Lt Wallace A. Bell L/5th RFA	
"	"	2/Lieut N. Hogan Gaul to 45th Bde RFA.	

Army Form C. 2118.

WAR DIARY
or
INTELLIGENCE SUMMARY.
(Erase heading not required.)

Instructions regarding War Diaries and Intelligence Summaries are contained in F. S. Regs., Part II. and the Staff Manual respectively. Title pages will be prepared in manuscript.

Hour, Date, Place	Summary of Events and Information	Remarks and references to Appendices
Nov 28th to 29th	8th Div moved back to rest in vicinity of BLARINGHEM, Div remained at POULIEU. Book Depot to BOIS des HUIT RUES	
30th	2.U.T.D. Welsh to 129th Howr. Bde	

J.H. Winter Wood
Capt D.A.A.C.

8th, Division.

8th, D. A. C.

December, 1915.

Sir Dinshaw Manackji Petit.

See
vol XIII

4946/
／101

WAR DIARY
or
INTELLIGENCE SUMMARY.
(Erase heading not required.)

Army Form C. 2118.

Hour, Date, Place	Summary of Events and Information	Remarks and references to Appendices
DOULIEU 17.12.15	2nd Lt. K.N. McClelland attached 335/78 Bde efflat from 9th and 2nd AR Welby attached to 8th BAC from	
" 14.12.15	Lieut G.C. Taylor arrived from 9th Div	
" 18.12.15	2/Lt. H. Eaton returned to No. 1 Section	
" " "	Lt. G.C. Tylor took over duties of Adjutant	
" 20.12.15	The 8th D.A.C. moved out to join the Division for manoeuvres, spent the night 20th, 21st in billets in MORBECQUE, where Bomb Depot rejoined	
MORBECQUE 21.12.15	8th D.A.C. moved to billets at WITTES, but owing to 1st place being full was afterwards ordered to move on to ROQUETOIRE, where they spent night of 21st 22nd HQ at CHATEAU DE LA MORANDE	
ROQUETOIRE 22.12.15.	Moved back to billets at MORBECQUE for night of 22nd 23rd	
MORBECQUE 23.12.15.	8th D.A.C. moved back to DOULIEU, reoccupying same billets they had left on 20.12.15. Bomb Depot returned at BOIS DES HUIT RUES.	
DOULIEU 26.12.15	Captain D.A. BUCHAN and Captain T.H. DAVISON joined 8th DAC.	

Army Form C. 2118.

WAR DIARY
or
INTELLIGENCE SUMMARY.
(Erase heading not required.)

Hour, Date, Place	Summary of Events and Information	Remarks and references to Appendices
DOULIEU. 26-12-15.	Captain D.A. Buchan posted to 5th Bde R.H.A.	
" " "	Captain T.H. Davison posted to 33rd Bde R.F.A.	
" " "	Captain Q.L. Borradaile posted to 8th D.A.C, but reported sick so did not join.	

A.M.Webster Colonel
Comdg 8th D.A.C.

8th, Division.

8th, D. A. C.

January, 1916.

Army Form C. 2118.

WAR DIARY
or
INTELLIGENCE SUMMARY.
(Erase heading not required.)

8 Divl Amn Column

Hour, Date, Place	Summary of Events and Information	Remarks and references to Appendices
1916		
DOULIEU 7-1-16	No 1 Section moved from their billet at BLEU to a new billet at F.22.c.9.4 on the road LE VERRIER — BLEU, old billet being required for infantry use during relief.	
13-1-16	8th Division took over from the 20th Division, thus coming into the line again.	
17-1-16	Captain M. MUIR STEWART joined the DAC from the Base & was posted to No 1 Section.	
18-1-16.	Captain L.E. FAGAN attached posted to No 3 Section from 33rd B.A.C. Lt R. McL. HUNTER attached posted to 33rd B.A.C.	
23-1-16.	2/Lt C.G.Q. NICHOLSON posted to 2 Battery R.H.A.	
30-1-16	Captain L.E. FAGAN posted to 8th D.A.C. Captain R. McL. HUNTER returns to 8th D.A.C. Captain E. SHERLOCK posted to 5th B'de R.H.A with effect from 1-2-16.	

Commanding 8° Divn Amn Col —

<u>8th, Division.</u>

<u>8th, D. A. C.</u>

<u>February, 1916.</u>

WAR DIARY or INTELLIGENCE SUMMARY

Army Form C. 2118.

Hour, Date, Place	Summary of Events and Information	Remarks and references to Appendices
	8 D.A.C.	
DOULIEU 1-2-16 February	Lt. C. STUART attached to 46th Bde RFA. 2/Lt G.H. HEDLEY to 5th Bde R.H.A.	
	2/Lt HEATON to 33rd Bde R.F.A. 2/Lt H.R. HOWES to 45th Bde R.F.A. 2/Lt C.B. GOLDING to 46th Bde R.F.A.	
	Lt H. BOTTOMLEY attached to 8th D.A.C. for duty at Boul. Depot from 33rd D.A.C.	
	2/Lt J.A.D. ROSS attached to 8th D.A.C. from 5th Bde R.H.A.	
	2/Lt S. SIMMONS attached to 8th D.A.C. from 33rd Bde R.F.A.	
	2/Lt HORGAN-GAUL returns to 8th D.A.C. from 33rd Bde R.F.A.	
	2/Lt A.R. totilly returns to 8th D.A.C. from 128th Bde R.F.A.	
5-2-16	No. 1 Section handed over Tipcars & H.D. horses at Thenouanne, receiving G.S. waggons and mules in steed.	
9-2-16	Dump of 378 Rds pergun 18 Pr & 40 Rds pergun 4.5 Howitzer made at respective B.A.C. No. 3 Section handed over Ypreants & H.D. horses at Thenouanne receiving of G.S. waggons and mules instead.	
10-2-16	Capt R.A. Lloyd-Barrow leaves 8 D.A.C. to be attached to 1st Army School of Mortars. Q.S.M. A.E. Redhead 8th D.A.C. to Gazetted 2nd Lieut. Lt. Col. 6/2/16. Left 8 D.A.C. for the Base on	

Army Form C. 2118.

WAR DIARY
or
INTELLIGENCE SUMMARY.
(Erase heading not required.)

Instructions regarding War Diaries and Intelligence Summaries are contained in F.S. Regs., Part II. and the Staff Manual respectively. Title pages will be prepared in manuscript.

Hour, Date, Place	Summary of Events and Information	Remarks and references to Appendices
DOUDEU. 10.2.16.	Promotion to 2nd Lieut. dated 6/2/16.	
13-2-16.	No. 2 Sectn handed over Tip-carts & 4 D horses at THEROUANNE receiving G.S. wagons & mules in place.	
18-2-16.	2/Lt S. STEWARDES attached to R.F.C. from 8th D.A.C.	
19.2-16.	2/Lt H. EATON returned to 8th D.A.C. from 33rd Bt RFA	
21-2-16	2/Lt S. SIMMONS posted to 8th D.A.C. and attached to R.F.C.	
	2/Lt R.N. GILBERT posted to 32nd Battery, vice 2/Lt S Simmons.	
24-2-16.	Wire received "Dump Am'n for Itao." Accordingly 100 Rds per 18 Pr and 75 Rds per gun 4.5 Howitzer were dumped.	
27-2-16.	Wire received "Adopt Itao precautions" Action taken accordingly.	

M. F. Peterston (?)
Lt Col
C.R.A 17th (?)

29-2-16

8th, Division.

8th, D. A. C.

March, 1916.

Instructions regarding War Diaries and Intelligence Summaries are contained in F. S. Regs., Part II. and the Staff Manual respectively. Title pages will be prepared in manuscript.

WAR DIARY
or
INTELLIGENCE SUMMARY.
(Erase heading not required.)

Army Form C. 2118.

Hour, Date, Place	Summary of Events and Information	Remarks and references to Appendices
[illegible] DIVISIONAL [illegible]		
DIVIDED [illegible]		
[illegible] 1916	2nd [illegible] [illegible] to [illegible] 3rd [illegible]	
	2nd [illegible] to [illegible] D A C	
6th 1916	Capt [illegible] to 5 D A C	
12th 1916	2nd [illegible] to [illegible]	
	to [illegible] B R F A	
27th 1916	[illegible]	
	[illegible] to BELLOY [illegible]	
	[illegible]	
[illegible] 3 16	[illegible] No 1 Sect [illegible] at LESTREM [illegible]	
	[illegible] to BELLOY	
	[illegible] 3 16	
"	[illegible] No 1 Section [illegible] LESTREM [illegible] pm [illegible] at BELLOY	
	[illegible] 3 16	
	[illegible] No 2 Section [illegible] at LESTREM 7 8 pm [illegible]	
	at BELLOY [illegible] 3 16	
	[illegible] No 2 Sect [illegible] at MERVILLE [illegible] at BELLOY 1 15 pm [illegible] 3 16	

(9 29 6) W 2794 100,000 8/14 H W V Forms/C. 2118/11.

Army Form C. 2118.

WAR DIARY
or
INTELLIGENCE SUMMARY.
(Erase heading not required.)

Instructions regarding War Diaries and Intelligence Summaries are contained in F. S. Regs., Part II. and the Staff Manual respectively. Title pages will be prepared in manuscript.

8th. Div. Ammn. Column.

Hour, Date, Place	Summary of Events and Information	Remarks and references to Appendices
DOULIEU 30.3.16.	2/3 No 3 Section entrained at MERVILLE at 12.0 a.m. and arrived at BELLOY at 6 p.m 30.3.16. H.Q. 8 D.A.C. at Schoolhouse in BELLOY. H.Q. 8th Div. ᗺ R.A. at FRESSELLES.	

M.B. Sutherland

8th, Division.

8th, D? A. C.

April, 1916.

WAR DIARY
or
INTELLIGENCE SUMMARY.
(Erase heading not required.)

Army Form C. 2118.

Hour, Date, Place	Summary of Events and Information	Remarks and references to Appendices
APRIL 3-4-16 BELLOY. 7-4-16	8th D.A.C. 2/Lt Hogan Genl proceeded to Boulogne for Dental Treatment. Billeting Party (Lt Officer Sime) started at 9 a.m. for BAVELINCOURT. Column started at 12 midday, arriving BAVELINCOURT via VIGNACOURT, FRESSELLES, VILLERS BOCAGE at 8 p.m. Billets in BAVELINCOURT. HQ at CHATEAU. HQ RA at HENENCOURT. Also Bomb sectn.	
10-4-16	2/Lt J.M.D. Ross seems to be attached to 8DAC & proceed to 5th BX RHA. Capt G.L. Borrowdale invalided home to England & struck off strength 1/8 DAC.	
28-4-16	Captain R.A. Lloyd Barrow struck off strength 1/8 DAC on his posting to Z/34 T.M. Bctte	
17-4-16	2/Lt S.S. Simmons posted to RFC & struck off strength 1/8 DAC.	
21-4-16	Lt A. Quarry proceeded to 4th Army School of instruction in Trench Mortars.	
22-4-16	2/Lt G.W. McL. Henderson posted to 8th DAC from Base.	

WAR DIARY
or
INTELLIGENCE SUMMARY.
(Erase heading not required.)

Army Form C. 2118.

Hour, Date, Place	Summary of Events and Information	Remarks and references to Appendices
	8th D.A.C.	
BAVELINCOURT 28-4-16	Lt QUARRY rejoined 8th D.A.C. from course instruction at 4th Army Trench Mortar School.	
29-4-16	Lt QUARRY left 8 D.A.C. to be attached to Y/8 Trench Mortar Battery.	
		J.B. Montherin Major C.y 8th D.A.C.

8th, Division.

8th, D. A. C.

May, 1916.

Army Form C. 2118.

WAR DIARY
or
INTELLIGENCE SUMMARY.
(Erase heading not required.)

Instructions regarding War Diaries and Intelligence Summaries are contained in F.S. Regs., Part II. and the Staff Manual respectively. Title pages will be prepared in manuscript.

Hour, Date, Place	Summary of Events and Information	Remarks and references to Appendices
	8. D.A.C.	
BAVELINCOURT. MAY 1916.		
9.5.16.	2/Lt H. EATON took over duties of Adjutant.	
10.5.16.	Orders received that B.A.C's should be absorbed into D.A.C. (Surplus horsepower & personnel evacuated).	
12.5.16.	Lt C. STUART posted to 45th B'de R.F.A. from 8 D.A.C.	
	2/Lt H HOWES posted to 45th B'de R.F.A. from 8 D.A.C.	
	2/Lt R.L. JUPP posted to 33rd B'de R.F.A. " "	
	2/Lt F.L. LEE posted to 33rd B'de R.F.A. " "	
	2/Lt T.D. WELDON posted to 128th B'de R.F.A. " "	
15-5-16.	Following Officers posted to 8 D.A.C.	
	Brig./Major	
	Captain C.E. VIVIAN, Lt E.C. MILLER from 45th B'de R.F.A.	
	Captain F.E.P. COWAN, 2/Lt H.K. BRIGGS from 128th B'de R.F.A.	
	Captain R McL HUNTER, Lt A.E.G. CHAMPION, Lt H. BOTTOMLEY from 33rd B'de R.F.A.	
	Captain M. BALFOUR, 2/Lt C.N. SILVESTER, 2/Lt C. ELLIS from 5th B'de R.H.A.	

WAR DIARY
INTELLIGENCE SUMMARY.
(Erase heading not required.)

Army Form C. 2118.

Hour, Date, Place	Summary of Events and Information	Remarks and references to Appendices
	8. D.A.C.	
BAVELINCOURT. 17.5.16.	HQ No.1 & No.3 Sections moved to BAISIEUX taking over Transport & personnel of 5th Bde R.H.A. A.C. & 33rd B.A.C.	
BAISIEUX	B Echelon began to form, composed of surplus Transport & personnel of B.A.C.s & Sections of D.A.C.	
19.5.16.	No. 2 Section Remained at BAVELINCOURT, where they were joined by 45th B.A.C. Temporary Section formed at BAVELINCOURT under Captain BALFOUR & these were selected for duty with French Motor Batteries.	
20-5-16	Lt. H. BOTTOMLEY marched to ABBEVILLE in charge of Transport & personnel for evacuation to Base. 18 G.S. wagons 3 Carts, 99 animals. 126 O.R.	
23-5-16	5 G.S. wagons handed over to 8th Div' han.	
23-24/5/16	12 G.S. wagons evacuated by horse from MERICOURT.	
	New Establishment. H.Q. 9 Vehicles 29 Officers 35 Horses.	

WAR DIARY
or
INTELLIGENCE SUMMARY.

(Erase heading not required.)

Army Form C. 2118.

8. D.A.C.

Hour, Date, Place	Summary of Events and Information	Remarks and references to Appendices
BAISIEUX. MAY.	New Establt (Cav). 9 Officers.	
	Nos 1, 2 & 3 Sections /2 105 Vehicles. 513 O.R. 484 horses. 155 mules	
	B Echelon. 46 Mules. 51 Vehicles. 239 O.R. 81	
	Total Column Excluding Attached. 260 O.R. 336 Mules 26 horses	
	Officers. 15. 168 Vehicles. 802 O.R. 1005 horses.	
27-5-16.	The following transfers & postings of Officers took place.	
	No 1 Section Captain R. McL HUNTER. LT PALMER. 2/LT SYLVESTER.	
	No 3 — Captain C.E. VIVIAN. 2/LT MILLER. 2/LT EATON.	
	B. ECHELON Captain. M. MUIR STEWART. 2/LT WELBY. 2/LT ELLIS	
29-5-16.	Captain F.E. COWAN & 2/LT AR WELBY. went on a Course in Trench Mortars to Y/8 Trench Mortar Battery.	

M. Butcherjohnd
Cmdg 8" D.A.C.

8th, Division.

8th, D. A. C.

June, 1916.

WAR DIARY
or
INTELLIGENCE SUMMARY.
(Erase heading not required.)

Army Form C. 2118.

8 Div Am Col

Hour, Date, Place	Summary of Events and Information	Remarks and references to Appendices
JUNE 6th BAISIEUX	8 D.A.C.	
7th	B ECHELON moved to position behind HENENCOURT WOOD. Headquarters & Nº 1, 2 & 3 sections moved to fields south west of MILLENCOURT. Headquarters in the village.	
8th	Dump began of 850 rounds per gun, which with the 150 rounds per gun already collected by emptying DAC A echelon & adding to existing Dumps at the guns. Ammunition refilling point established just outside Henencourt on the HENENCOURT — LAVIEVILLE road. 2/Lt EATON in charge 35 GS wagons sent up the first night with (Corps) Ammn.	
10th	Lt G.S. BARROW posted to 45th Bde. 2/Lt J.E. HUMBERSTONE posted to 8th DAC.	
9 – 13th	DAC helped to carry Amm to Batteries of 45th Bde & Z, who were at Mackie Camp, & had only one section in action.	
16th	DAC vehicles were filled up, thus carrying 76 rds per gun 18 p's & 48 rds per gun 4.5' Howitzers.	
17th	Dump completed, and Batteries refilled all Echelons.	

Army Form C. 2118.

WAR DIARY
or
INTELLIGENCE SUMMARY.
(Erase heading not required.)

Instructions regarding War Diaries and Intelligence Summaries are contained in F. S. Regs., Part II. and the Staff Manual respectively. Title pages will be prepared in manuscript.

Place	Hour, Date	Summary of Events and Information	Remarks and references to Appendices
MILLENCOURT	14-6-16	8. D.A.C.	
	22-6-16	CAPT. L.E. FAGAN R.F.A. Struck off strength of 8th Div. A.T.C.	
		2/Lt C.M SYLVESTER Attached to 5th Bde R.F.A.	
		2/Lt H.K BRIGGS " 45th – R.F.A	
	26-6-16	Captain F.E.P. COWAN Struck off strength & posting to v/8 T.M. Battery with effect from 4-6-16.	
	22-6-16	Half establishment of gun stores held by D.A.C. distributed to Brigade	
	24-6-16	Ammunition sent up to Bde as follows 33rd Bde	
	25-6-16		A	AX	BX
		45th "	2052	684	240
		5th "	2052	684	240
		5th "	1368	456	240
		33rd "	2052	684	
	26-6-16	" "	1995	665	320
		45th "			320
		5th "	1311	437	
		33rd "	2052	684	160
	27-6-16	45th "	2052	684	160
		6th "	1368	456	160

WAR DIARY
or
INTELLIGENCE SUMMARY

(Erase heading not required.)

Army Form C. 2118

Place	Date	Hour	Summary of Events and Information	Remarks and references to Appendices
MILLENCOURT	28.6.16		& D.A.C. Ammunition Supplies to Brigades.	
			By A Echelon By B Echelon.	
			A AX BX A AX BX	
			33rd Bde. 2840 796 384 33rd. 1684 584 256	
			45th 2840 796 384 45th 1684 584 256	
			5th R.H.A. 1893 531 384 5th R.H.A. 1684 1124 376 256	
"	29th		33rd 2700 900 720	
			45th 2700 900 720	
			5th R.H.A. 1800 600 720	
"	30th		" 33rd 3078 1026 576 1647 549 424	
			45th 3078 1026 576 1647 549 424	
			5th R.H.A. 2052 684 576 1098 366 424	
			Six Officers joined from Base.	
			Lt. HERBERT REYNOLDS. 2/Lt. HAROLD NEWTON KING.	
			2/Lt. DAVID STRACHAN. 2/Lt. TOM ANTONY MICKALLI.	
			2/Lt. ERNEST VICTOR MORGAN. 2/Lt. FRED LEACH.	

I. Corps.
First Army.

Division transferred
from III. Corps,
Fourth Army, 8.7.16.

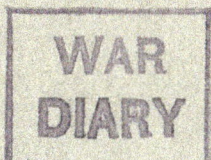

8th DIVISION AMMUNITION COLUMN.

J U L Y

1 9 1 6

30-7-16

A G's Office
        Base

Herewith War Diary
for 8th Div'l Am'n
Column for month
of July 1916.

G C Tyler R.F.A
Adjt for OC 8 DAC

Army Form C. 2118
8 D Amm Col
Vol 2 D

WAR DIARY
or
INTELLIGENCE SUMMARY

(Erase heading not required.)

Place	Date	Hour	Summary of Events and Information	Remarks and references to Appendices
MILLENCOURT	1-7-16		Ammunition supplied to Brigades during the offensive.	
			A AX TSX	
			33rd Bde 1026 342	
			45th - 780 274	
			5th - R.H.A. 684 1236	
	2/7/6			
			33rd Bde 5331 1777 384	
			45th - 2960 990	
			5th - R.H.A. 2284 984 384	
			Following Officers joined from Base	
			2/Lt. IAN GEOFFREY BRASSEY	
			2/Lt. CHARLES EDWARD LARGE.	
			A AX 13X	
	3/7/6		33rd 2264 717 432	
			45th - 2048 526 288	
			5th - RHA 412 500 1228	
			Infantry of 18th Division marched back to rest being relieved by infantry of 12th Bgde Division. During all these operations we handled over 3000 Tons of 18 pr & 4.5" ammunition, this does not include a vast quantity of T.M. amm. and grenades.—	

Army Form C. 2118

WAR DIARY
or
INTELLIGENCE SUMMARY
(Erase heading not required.)

Instructions regarding War Diaries and Intelligence Summaries are contained in F.S. Regs., Part II. and the Staff Manual respectively. Title Pages will be prepared in manuscript.

Place	Date	Hour	Summary of Events and Information	Remarks and references to Appendices
			8. D.A.C.	
MILLENCOURT	4-7-16		8th D.A.C. moved at 10 a.m. to BAVELINCOURT, being relieved by 12th D.A.C.	
BAVELINCOURT	5-7-16		8th D.A.C. " at 12 midday to CROUY. arriving about 9 p.m.	
CROUY	6-7-16		HQ & 8th D.A.C. moved at 12 midnight to SALEUX (where they entrained).	
	7-7-16		Arriving BRYAS at 2 p.m., @ AUCHEL at 5 p.m.	
			No 1 Section left LONGUEAU by train at 2.30 p.m., arrived at AUCHEL via PERNES at 1 a.m. 8-7-16.	
			" 2 " " " " " " " " 8.30 p.m. " " AUCHEL " PERNES at 7.30 a.m. 8-7-16	
			" 3 " " " " " " " " 9.30 p.m. " " AUCHEL " DEVAL at 11 a.m. 8-7-16	
			" 3½ - 4 " " " " " " 10.30 p.m. " " AUCHEL " BRYAS " 10 a.m. 8-7-16	
			" ½ - 4 " " " " " " 11.30 p.m. " " AUCHEL " PERNES " 10.30 " 8-7-16	
	8-7-16		Details (1,203) " " " " " " 12.30 a.m. " " AUCHEL " DEVAL " " 8-7-16	
AUCHEL			Lt ALEXANDER ANSON McLEOD R.F.A. T. ⎫	
			2/Lt SAMUEL LESLIE BIBBY. " " ⎬ Joined from Base.	
			2/Lt JAMES PERCIVAL BISHOP. " " ⎪	
			2/Lt GEORGE RONALD PYM BROWN " " ⎭	
	10-7-16		Joined from Base 2/Lt NORRYS AUBREY BEST (T.F.)	

WAR DIARY
or
INTELLIGENCE SUMMARY
(Erase heading not required.)

Army Form C. 2118

Place	Date	Hour	Summary of Events and Information	Remarks and references to Appendices
AUCHEL	13-7-16		8 D.A.C. GOC 8th Division inspected the Column, making a very complimentary speech on the work done by the Column in the recent operations, and for thirty to two men per return were carried out.	
"	14-7-16		DAC marched at 7.30 a.m. to CROIX MARMUSE, leaving behind at AUCHEL the small arms & grenade sections. This was due to fact that infantry did not march with Division with but remained in rest.	
NOUVEAU MONDE	15-7-16		DAC moved into position at G 27 D on Nouveau Monde — Sailly road, while the Batteries moved up into wire cutting positions in front of LAVENTIE.	
	16-7-16		Ice was necessary to be ready to receive Ammunition by 2 p.m., but the first supply did not arrive till 2.30 a.m. Dump of 600 Rounds per gun 18pr & 166 per gun 4.5" howitzer was continued. During the day supply of Ammunition from Parks was very slow indeed. By 6 a.m. we managed to complete the Dump to refill B.A.C., but only by means of keeping all men & teams hard at work all night.	
	17-7-16		Posted to Brigades as under—	
			To 5th Bde R.H.A. Lt. A.A. McLEOD R.F.A. To 45th Bde R.F.A. 2/Lt G.W. HENDERSON. R.F.A.	
			Lt. H. REYNOLDS — 2/Lt D. STRACHAN. —	
			2/Lt F. LEACH. — 2/Lt. E.V. MORGAN —	
			2/Lt. C.N. SYLVESTER — 2/Lt H.K. BRIGGS —	
	18-7-16		To 33rd Bde R.F.A. Lt J. SMITH R.F.A	
			2/Lt T.A. MCKALLS -	
			2/Lt H.V. KING -	
			2/Lt I.G. BRASSEY -	

WAR DIARY
or
INTELLIGENCE SUMMARY

Army Form C. 2118

Place	Date	Hour	Summary of Events and Information						Remarks and references to Appendices
			8th D.A.C.		A	AX	BX		
NOUVEAU MONDE	17-7-16		By 6 a.m. we had sent up the following ammunition	45th/13th R.F.A.	8100	2700	664		
				33rd/13th R.F.A.	8100	2700	664		
				5th – R.H.A.	5400	1800	90		
	18-7-16		Sent up the following ammunition so as to bring	45th/13th R.F.A.	3871	648	175		
			Dump & Guns up to original strength	33rd – "	2551	365	98		
				5th – R.H.A.	1026	84			
	19-7-16		Attack having been postponed on evening of 18th	45th R.F.A.	414		460		
			we sent up to replace expenditure.	33rd "	748	12	257		
				5th R.H.A.	121	342	342		
			Attack took place at 7 p.m. in the evening & before that time the Germans had been shelling our batteries heavily, so that during that time we had to send up as follows: Nº 20 guns to 32nd Battery @ 6 to 45th Bde.						
			Ammunition sent up	45th 13th 12 F.A.	792	– 264			
				33rd – R.F.A.	2429	– 490	440		
				5th – R.H.A.	2996	– 852	336		
	20-7-16		Throughout these 5 days supply of Ammunition to DAC was extraordinarily slow. Batteries were like in a great deficiency in supply, so that we had all our work cut out to keep pace with issues. I could never get up to strength. Ammunition we believed to be mostly from 61st Div's Dump, but also by 8th A.S.P. & 39 G. ASP, who collected it from there & our DAC to try & supply us. It came from every source, a few lorry loads at a time & made the supply a very difficult affair. It was remarkable how supply on this occasion differed from that of 3rd Corps 4th Army, which was very well arranged, though there were heavy amounts.						

Army Form C. 2118

WAR DIARY
or
INTELLIGENCE SUMMARY
(Erase heading not required.)

Instructions regarding War Diaries and Intelligence Summaries are contained in F. S. Regs., Part II. and the Staff Manual respectively. Title Pages will be prepared in manuscript.

8th D.A.C.

Place	Date	Hour	Summary of Events and Information	Remarks and references to Appendices
NOUEAU MONDE	20-7-16		2/Lt A.R Welby attached Y/8 Trench Mortar Battery wounded in arm & sent to hospital. During this period we had to supply a working party of 75 men to Brigade, of whom 4 were wounded. There was no respite of time for unloading & loading Ammunition until mended. The Battalion returned to us. During night of 20th & following Day most of this Amm was unloaded, & so we had to work all day very hard to get it reloaded, as we moved at 7.30 p.m. On moving we handed over to 61st D.A.C. The column moved at 7.30 p.m. arriving at Foxe No 2	A 13756 AX 4407 BX 1559 A 14566 AX 5272 BX 391
ANNEZIN	22-7-16		D'ANNEZIN at 12.30 a.m. Column moved to VERQUIGNEUL, last section arriving at 7 p.m. Sections billeted as follows. No 1 & 2 Sections HQ in VERQUIGNEUL No 3 Section at BEUVRY. B Echelon at FOUQUIÈRES. Horse lines ludged in all places. Billets good. Handed over to 15th D.A.C. when we relieved A.Q.R.A at SAILLY LABOURSE	A 2844 AX 596 BX 1163
VERQUIGNEUL	24-7-16		Posted to 45th By RFA. 2/Lt C.E. LARGE. RFA. " to 33rd Div. Lt AEG CHAMPION. RFA. " to 33rd By. Lt J SMITH. RFA. Struck off strength on evacuation to England wounded. 2/Lt A.R WELBY. RFA.	

1875. Wt. W593/826 1,000,000 4/15 J.B.C. & A. A.D.S.S./Forms/C. 2118.

Army Form C. 2118

WAR DIARY
or
INTELLIGENCE SUMMARY

(Erase heading not required.)

Instructions regarding War Diaries and Intelligence Summaries are contained in F. S. Regs., Part II. and the Staff Manual respectively. Title Pages will be prepared in manuscript.

Place	Date	Hour	Summary of Events and Information	Remarks and references to Appendices
VERQUIGNEUL			8 DAC.	
	26-7-16		Under arrangements made by I. Corp establishment of Amm'n now as follows. A&Ax B&x
			At Guns 252 174
			Wagon line 102 88
			DAC. ASP } NIL NIL
			Total 354 262
	27-7-16		2/Lt F LEACH is posted to 8th DAC. from 6th Bde R.H.A.
	29-7-16		At 10.30 p.m. S.O.S. message received. DAC did not turn out but stood by with wagons full ready to deliver Am'n. It was all over at 1 a.m., very little Am'n being demanded.

A.M.Sellater Colonel
(Cmd) 8 D.A.C.

8th, Division.

8th, D. A. C.

August, 1916.

CONFIDENTIAL.

8th DIVISIONAL ARTILLERY.

WAR DIARY

OF

8th Divn Amm. Column

From 1-8-16 To 31-8-16

(VOLUME 21)

With APPENDICES Nos. None

Vol 21

WAR DIARY or INTELLIGENCE SUMMARY

Army Form C. 2118

(Erase heading not required.)

Place	Date	Hour	Summary of Events and Information	Remarks and references to Appendices
VERQUIGNEUL	1-8-16		LT A. QUARRY struck off strength with effect from 28-7-16 on posting to Y/5 T.M. Battery.	G.C.T.
	5-8-16		B Echelon moved from FOUQUIERES to billets in VERQUIGNEUL	G.C.T.
	–		2/LT N. MORGAN GAUL struck off strength with effect from 26-6-16.	G.C.T.
	12-8-16		New scheme of Ammunition supply came into force, to effect further economy in petrol. Div¹ Column to draw Ammunition & grenades etc from railhead & Bomb store except in cases of Emergency when lorries from Park are brought into use. Indent submitted to A.S.P. as usual.	G.C.T.
	13-8-16		D.A.C. when D.when Ammunition required is available. Shells dropped just outside village. Our Enemy shelled VERQUIGNEUL tonight about 20 rounds. 1 shell near 3rd gun of 4th gun, man 3rd gun slightly wounded. B Echelon 2/LT R.R. BROWN & 2/LT J ELLIS on posting to French Mortar Battalion.	Q.C.T.
	15-8-16		New instructions issued re reinforcements of Trench Mortar Batteries. All such to be posted from the Div¹ Ammun Column, who will demand from Base Days to refill. Trench Mortar Batteries to submit A.F.B. 213 weekly to the D.A.C.	G.C.T.
	16-8-16		Dvr 16 1 Officer & 24 O.R joined from Base. Six of these were R.H.A Telephonists.	G.C.T.
			LV IAN BOTTOMLEY posted to Nº 3 Section.	G.C.T.
			B Echelon moved into Waggon Line previously occupied by 3rd B.Gh Waggon Line.	G.C.T.
	27-8-16		2/LT G.H. HEDLEY posted to 33rd BRIGADE vice 2/LT F.E. FRITH posted to 8th D.A.C. for Duty at Bomb Depot.	G.C.T.
	31-8-16		CAPT M. BALFOUR 8th D.A.C., attached Trench Mortar Battery, is attached to 45th Bde R.F.A. Ammunition supply again changed. Ammun¹ brought by rail from LAPUGNOY to BEUVRY HALT, where it is collected by various D.A.C's. Quite successful. Took just under half an hour loading up with 2000 A.X.	Q.C.T.
	28-8-16		Twenty officers & 74 O.R arrived at VERQUIGNEUL, surplus personnel of 16th Division, & were attached to 8th D.A.C. pending instructions as to their disposal.	G.C.T.

AM Letupham
(Major) D.A.C.

8th, Division.

8th, D. A. C.

September, 1916.

CONFIDENTIAL.

8th DIVISIONAL ARTILLERY.

WAR DIARY

OF

8th Division. Amⁿ. Column.

From 1st Sept. 1916. To 30° Sept. 1916.

(VOLUME ~~XXIII~~)

With APPENDICES Nos. NONE.

Vol 22

WAR DIARY
or
INTELLIGENCE SUMMARY

(Erase heading not required.)

Army Form C. 2118

Place	Date	Hour	Summary of Events and Information	Remarks and references to Appendices
VERQUIGNEUL	September 9th		8 D.A.C. 6 Officers of 16th Div. attached 8th D.A.C. attached to Batteries 2/Lt T.W. Dean to C Battery 2/Lt A.B. Lythgoe to 45th BDE " 2/Lt J.T. Richards to 33rd BDE " C.F. Lushington " " " G.L. Maslen " 33rd " — Capt. G.C. Nugent to 33rd BDE " J.R. Hagarty " 33rd " —	G.C.T.
	10th		All the Officers of 16 Div ordered to return to their Division with the exception of Lt. Col. Cochrane, who joined 1st Division. Following Officers posted to 8 D.A.C. from 63rd R.N. Division. *Lieut. William Hendrey Don R.F.A. " 2/Lieut. Waller Waller Wilkinson — " Lieut. Cecil Miller — " 2/ — James Noel Green — "	G.C.T.
	12th		— Cynodlan Jones — " — William Perceval Gair — " — William Rowe — " — William Hunter — " Following posted to Brigades. 45th BDE R.F.A. 33rd BDE R.F.A. 5th BDE R.H.A. 2/Lt W.P. Gair R.F.A. 2/Lt I.N. Green R.F.A. 2/Lt W.W. Wilkinson R.F.A. 2/Lt W. Rowe — 2/Lt C. Jones " 2/Lt W. Hunter "	
	13th		Arrangement for Supply of Ammunition again changed. Divisionally allotment to make amount due to Corps to Dawn from VERQUIGNEUL Railhead by Sub Park Lorries & dumped at site selected in DROUVIN - NOEUX LES G.C.T. MINES Road (Sheet 36 B K 11) Thence it to Dawn by D.A.C. as ordered by _____ 4/15 J.B.C. & A M A.D.S.S./Forms/C. 2118. G.O.C. R.A. no present.	

WAR DIARY
or
INTELLIGENCE SUMMARY

Army Form C. 2118

Place	Date	Hour	Summary of Events and Information	Remarks and references to Appendices
VERQUIGNEUL	September			
	17th		8.D.A.C.	
			1 Water Cart & 2 horses 8/6 Div sent to 3rd Divl Train for use of Commandant Prisoner of War Coy	
	18th		2/Lt BIBBY started for THEROUANNE with remainder of surplus vehicles 8.D.A.C. & horses on arrival there he had to take transport on to ABBEVILLE & hand over to Commandant there. This consisted of 2 Water Carts, 1 Telephone Cart, 6 Cooks Cars, 1 Maltese Cart	G.C.T.
	23rd		3 G.S. wagons surplus stores 8/6 D.A. returned to O.A.D.O.S. 8 Div.	G.C.T.
	24th		Special decine opened at the rate of 1 per week for the D.A.C.	G.C.T.

Commdg 8th D.A.C.

8th, Division.

8th, D. A. C.

October, 1916.

CONFIDENTIAL.

8th DIVISIONAL ARTILLERY.

WAR DIARY

OF

8º Dwn Am Col

From 1-10-16 To 31-10-16

(VOLUME 24)

With APPENDICES Nos.

WAR DIARY or INTELLIGENCE SUMMARY

Army Form C. 2118

Place	Date	Hour	Summary of Events and Information	Remarks and references to Appendices
Haquemont Octobre	12th		6 D.A.C. Instructions 1st 8th Div ordered by 21st Div to sent by rail to Longpré (followed by ...)	GCT
	12/13/21st		proceed to training area at FRIVILLERS. Bomb section completed there. All time our R.T. posts at 8, 13, 14 + 15 R	GCT
			DAC united all echelons at OXA till arrival of Advance party with HQ 1 section per battery.	GCT
	22nd	2 pm	All ammunition supplies to British loaded over AQUA AX 1184. Columns headed to billets at LABOURIÈRE HQ R.A. at MARLES-LES-MINES	GCT
Labourière	23rd	9 am	Arrived in billets at 5 pm. Columns balanced. Work going on at HEUCHIN & FONTAINE LES BOULANS at 4.30 pm HQRA at AUXI	GCT
Heuchin	24th	9 am	March continued. Column arrived at ETRÉE WAMIN & BERLENCOURT at 3.30 p.m. Very hot all day	GCT
Etrée Wamin	25th	9.30 am	March continued to AMPLIER & ORVILLE via BEAUVOIR - LUCHEUX - HALLOY. Billets. One section Horse & Amplier - arriving in billets at 2 pm	GCT
Orville	26th	9 am	DAC billets at ORVILLE. HQRA at AMPLIER.	
			DAC headed to TALMAS via AUTHIEULE - HALLEUX - BEAUVAL - FIENVILLERS - LILLERS about 2 pm	GCT
Talmas	27th	6.30	DAC continued march to DACOURS via ROBECOURT - MOLLIENS AU BOIS - QUERRIEU arrived 11.30 at Village (arrived) first night in billets on which the Div Artillery were billeted there	GCT

WAR DIARY or INTELLIGENCE SUMMARY

Army Form C. 2118

Place	Date	Hour	Summary of Events and Information	Remarks and references to Appendices
DAOURS	28		8 D.A.C. Brigade went forward to CITADEL area leaving DAC in DAOURS	QCT
	29		Party of 1 Officer & 6 NCOs sent forward to CARNOY to take over Ammunition Dump & Camp P Equipment from 56th DAC.	QCT
	30		Change in Column — All details for supply of SAA combined into one Section, taking the place of B Echelon. All 18 p^r & 4.5" Howrs. wagons handed over to A Echelon. Establd. under new system — Each Section of A Echelon Officers 3 OR 175 LD 190 Q.F.wagons 20 B Echelon " 4 OR 247 LD 316 GS.9 H.Q. " 2 OR 31 LD 34 GS.bag 43 SAA Col.G. 15 GS.bag 4 GS.bag for Ammn Dumps forn	
	31		Advanced party of 12 men sent forward by lorry to take over Ammn Dumps from 56 DAC.	QCT

J.M.Littlejohn

(Capt) 8th D.A.C

8th, Division.

8th, D. A. C.

Novvembe r, 1916.

CONFIDENTIAL.

8th. DIVISIONAL ARTILLERY

WAR DIARY

OF

8th Div Am Column

From 1-11-16   To 30-11-16

(VOLUME ~~XXV~~)

With Appendices Nos. 2

WAR DIARY or INTELLIGENCE SUMMARY

Army Form C. 2118

Vol 24

Place	Date	Hour	Summary of Events and Information	Remarks and references to Appendices
November DAOURS	1st	7 a.m.	8 D.A.C. Column marched to CARNOY, route CORBIE, MERICOURT & FRICOURT. Found camp in a horrible state. Telephone wires laid anyhow & accommodation insufficient. No telephonic communication for 24 hours.	Q.C.T.
CARNOY	2nd	2 a.m.	Sent up 300 BX by pack arrival to Battery. During Day all horses in column except 20 were out. Some of them twice. Sending up Am'n from Railhead to Dump 2000 18Pr: 1000 BX.	Q.C.T.
	3rd	—	36 G.S. wagon loads of Am'n sent up to Dump from Railhead. Total of 3000 18Pr: 500 BX. Every other animal available used for packing Am'n up to Batteries, in all 500 Rds being sent up this way.	Q.C.T.
	4th		LT.R.B. NUNN R.F.A. & 2/LT J.M. UNDERWOOD, T.S. STIRLING, J.M.M. DODDS, D.M. THOMAS R.F.A. posted to D.A.C. Railhead practically empty & Dump overflowing, so only pack horses were used.	Q.C.T.
	5th 6th		2300 Rds sent up on packs 4/11 J.M. UNDERWOOD RFA, 2/LT J.S. STIRLING posted to 645 18Pr — 2/Lt D.M. THOMAS to 5th Bd R.H.A. 7000 Rds 18Pr & 4.5 Ammunition sent up on pack animals. Trucks getting very bad owing to continued rain. & 2 mules were drowned in a shell hole.	Q.C.T.
	7th		8th Div! Gy.R came into the line again on our front. B echelon as a complete S.A.A. section took over from 33rd Div. S.A.A. section. Congratulatory letter from 33rd Div! received with a covering letter from C.R.A. 8th Div! (Attached herewith).	Q.C.T.
	8th 9th		About 2000 Rds sent up to Guns on packs & an equal amount to Dump from Railhead	Q.C.T.

Army Form C. 2118

WAR DIARY
or
INTELLIGENCE SUMMARY
(Erase heading not required.)

Instructions regarding War Diaries and Intelligence Summaries are contained in F.S. Regs, Part II. and the Staff Manual respectively. Title Pages will be prepared in manuscript.

Place	Date	Hour	Summary of Events and Information	Remarks and references to Appendices
CONVOY.	10th		& D.A.C. About 4000 Rds 18Pr & 4.5 Sent up to Dump from railhead, & 3000 18Pr brought back to column, so as to enable us to load pack animals for first journey to gun position; making second journey from forward dump. The method being found 2 hours quicker than when loading twice at TROVES WOOD.	Q.C.T.
	11th		960 AD AX & 480 BX sent up on pack animals to Batteries up to DUMP.	Q.C.T.
	12th		160 AD AX sent up to Batteries on packs. 2560	Q.C.T.
	13th		LT. W.H. DON R.F.A. posted to 5th Bde. R.H.A.	Q.C.T.
	14th		1920 18Pr sent up on packs. 532A & 22 BX sent up to DUMP.	Q.C.T.
	15th		348 to J.L. sent up to DUMP.	Q.C.T.
	16th		680 AD AX sent up to Batteries on packs. Owing to dreadful state of Dump at TROVES WOOD, it was moved to GUILLEMONT STATION. LT PALMER relieved LT MILLER. Party of 24 NCOs & men to work Dump. Most ammunition to come up unboxed, boxes to be returned by rail from there.	Q.C.T.
	17th		LT C. MILLER R.F.A. & 2/LT ~~C~~ S.L. BIBBY posted to 33rd & 45th B des. Draft of 86 men to Brigades, leaving us under strength.	Q.C.T.

WAR DIARY
or
INTELLIGENCE SUMMARY

Army Form C. 2118

Place	Date	Hour	Summary of Events and Information	Remarks and references to Appendices
			8 D.A.C.	
CARNOY	16th		B Echelon on S.A.A. Section marched to CITADEL with 8th Div Infantry. Being relieved by 29th Division marched empty except for S.A.A. Carts to Grenade Wagon. 4R & 36 L.D. collected from Bernancourt. 1R & 6L.D. for D.A.C.	G.C.T.
	17th		In evening S.A.A. Section got order to return to D.A.C. with exception of 23 G.S. Wagons, which went to new area to help transport Infantry kits, & then G.C.T. returned to return on completion.	
	18th 19th		560 18P. Sent up a packs to guns. 800 AX allotted to us at DUMP. This was left for Batteries to collect. 310 18P. Sent up to guns. Then left D.A.C. with only 197 A & battery at GUILLEMONT STATION.	G.C.T. G.C.T.
	20th		B 2 echelon supply 12 G.S wagon daily for use of Heavy Artillery; 2 for K.G. Balloon Section & 1 for A.A. Battery. 193 wagon from each section in A. echelon sent to Brigades.	e.C.T.
	21st		11 Riders 89 L.D. 32 mules arrived at Edgehill D.A.C. kept 2R 32 mules 50 L.D. Remainder sent to Brigades. 197 A new to Z Battery on packs, emptying the D.A.C. completely.	
	22nd		All available G.S wagon sent out daily drawing material for Batteries from R.E. loop siding & delivery to wagon lines.	G.C.T.
	23rd			

WAR DIARY or INTELLIGENCE SUMMARY

Army Form C. 2118

(Erase heading not required.)

Place	Date	Hour	Summary of Events and Information	Remarks and references to Appendices
CARNOY	23-11-16		8 D.A.C. Operation Order No. 42 received. 8th Div Art'y to be transferred from XIV Corps to XV Corps Area by Route March. 8th D.A. to be relieved by portions of 17th & 20th D.A. All Amm'n to be handed over to relieving units; all echelons to march out empty, as a result all wagons & lorries to deliver any amm'n on hand at GUILLEMONT STATION, where a dump of 100 rds per gun 18pr. & 4.5" Howitzer had to be established.	
	26/17		Batteries began to be relieved by portions of 17th & 20th D.A.	G.C.T.
	27/28		Remainder of Batteries relieved. Dwilt. Drawn to Wagon Lines.	G.C.T.
	28		Dump at Guillemont taken over by 17 D.A. Lt. Palmer & party returned to D.A.C. Lt. Palmer & 1 N.C.O. per section sent on to HORNOY in lorry to arrange billets.	G.C.T.
BAOURI	29		D.A.C. marches to BAOURI starting at 2 a.m. Route CITADEL - BRAY. CORBIE road. Very dark & cold, but fine. Column arrived at DAOURS about 9.30 a.m. No billets & men had to Bivouac.	G.C.T.
	30		Column marched at 7 a.m. to LA CHAUSSÉE. Accommodation very good. Column arrived in billets at 11 a.m.	G.C.T.
			Comparative statement of Amm'n sent up by Brigades of D.A.C. attached.	

M. Peter Island
(Capt) 8" D.A.C.

/

SENT UP BY 8th D.A.C.

Date November	To Guns by Pack Horse.		To DUMP in G.S. Wagons.	
	18 p⁻	4.5" Howitzer.	18 p⁻	4.5" Howitzer
1st – 2nd	—	300	—	—
2nd – 3rd	800	200	3312	1124
3rd – 4th	2300	400	2400	666
4th – 5th	1100	1100	724	—
5th – 6th	5292	—	316	270
6th – 7th	1708	500	1000	730
7th – 8th	—	—	—	—
8th – 9th	2000	—	2000	300
9th – 10th	800	—	3600	448
10th – 11th	960	480	4110	800
11th – 12th	2560	—	—	200
12th – 13th	—	—	—	—
13th – 14th	1920	456	532	22
14th – 15th	—	—	—	—
15th – 16th	680	—	—	350
16th – 17th	—	—	—	—
17th – 18th	560	—	—	—
18th – 19th	310	—	—	—
19th – 20th	397	—	—	—
TOTAL	21,387 ˣ	3,436 ˣ	17,994 ⊕	4,910

⊕ In addition 2592 18p⁻ was drawn from Railhead & brought to DAC. This is included in total sent to guns.
ˣ 5476 18p⁻ & 1368 4.5" is included in this; this is Establ⁻ of DAC & the DUMP at DAC taken over from 56th DAC.

II.

As a comparison with sheet I the following amounts of Amm^n were sent up to guns by Battery Wagon lines.

Ammunition sent to guns by Wagon lines Nov. 1st to Nov. 20th.

5th Bde R.H.A.		33rd Bde			Bde R.F.A.		45th Bde R.F.A.			
"O"	"Z"	D/5	32	33	36	55	1	3	5	57
6054	4559	3500	5510	5710	3236	2181	5345	5213	3948	2413

8th D.A. No................

Officer Commanding,

    8th Divisional Ammunition Column.

    The C.R.A. forwards the attached with great pleasure.

    He wishes all ranks D.A.C. to be told that their hard work in getting up Ammunition has helped so considerably to bring about this fine performance.

                                              Major, R.A.

7-11-16.   Brigade Major, 8th Divl Arty.

The following telegram has been received by the
B.G.R.A., Right Artillery, which he has great pleasure in
communicating to all ranks.

He wishes to express at the same time his
appreciation of the way all ranks under his command have
worked throughout:-

"Brig. Gen. Prescott-Decie, REDOUBT

A.D. 35   6th.

The 33rd. Division thank you and all ranks of the Artillery
under your command for enabling them to advance AAA Your
fire killed most of the German defenders and caused the
others to run away.

            Major General PINNEY"

         D.C. Spencer-Smith Major
6/11/16.   Brigade Major 4th. Divisional Artillery

8th, Division.

8th, D. A. C.

December, 1916.

CONFIDENTIAL.

8th. DIVISIONAL ARTILLERY

WAR DIARY

OF

8° Div. Am Col

From 1.12.16. To 31.12.16.

(VOLUME XXVI)

With Appendices Nos.

Army Form C. 2118

WAR DIARY
or
INTELLIGENCE SUMMARY

(Erase heading not required.)

Instructions regarding War Diaries and Intelligence Summaries are contained in F. S. Regs., Part II. and the Staff Manual respectively. Title Pages will be prepared in manuscript.

8 D.A.C. Vol. 25.

Place	Date	Hour	Summary of Events and Information	Remarks and references to Appendices
LA CHAUSSÉE	1-12-16		Column moved at 7.30 a.m. to ANDAINVILLE. H.Q.R.A. at BEZENCOURT. H.Q. D.A.C. at BELLOY ST LEONARD. Long march. Cold. Billets good.	G.C.T.
	2-12-16		March continued to ANDAINVILLE by long march. A echelon D.A.C. in ANDAINVILLE. B Echelon in ANDAINVILLE – AUBERT. H.Q.R.A. in BEZENCOURT.	G.C.T.
ANDAINVILLE	3-12-16		D.A.C. inspected by G.O.C. 8th DIV., who congratulated the Column on their turn out.	G.C.T.
	5-12-16		No 3 Section moved at 8 a.m. to ARGOEUVRES (being part 8 Ammn with one battery from 45th @ 35th Brigades.	G.C.T.
	6-12-16		No 3 Section moved at 8.45 a.m. to VAUX-SUR-SOMME.	G.C.T.
	7-12-16		No 3 Section moved at noon to Camp 14.	G.C.T.
	8-12-16		H.Q. D.A.C. with B.wit, 1 Battery from 33rd B45th B.22 Brigade H.Q. moved to ARGOEUVRES. No 3 Section filled with Ammn at PLATEAU SIDING & returned to Camp 14.	G.C.T.
	9-12-16		H.Q. D.A.C. marched to VAUX. No 3 Section delivered 912 A.B. A.X. to 3rd @ 36th Battens. No 2 Section started march to ARGOEUVRES to pay returned to Amonbaull, VAUX. H.Q D.A.C. joined No 3 Section at Camp 14. No 2 Section marched to	G.C.T.
	10-12-16		which was very crowded. No 3 Section who had refilled at PLATEAU delivered 912 A.B. A.X.	G.C.T.
			B.3. B. B.36th Battens. No 1 Section marched to ARGOEUVRES with B.wit.	
	11-12-16		H.Q. @ 3 Section marched to Bronfay Farm. due to BRONFAY FARM in BRAY – HARDECOURT road. Accommodation very bad. Arrangements for allotting of huts was erratic. No 2 Section marched to Camp 14. No 1 Section marched to VAUX.	G.C.T.
	12-12-16		No 2 Section joined B wit @ joined HQ B.W. 3 section. No 1 Section marched to Camp 14, where it joined wit C.	
			Col. F.W. BOTELER RFA granted 14 months leave to England. Major L.B. MONTRESOR RFA took Command of the Column.	G.C.T.
BRONFAY FARM	13-12-16		No 3 Section delivered to 3rd B36 B.tn 684 A 228 AX. No 1 Section marched to BRONFAY FARM & occupied hut at Camp 108 temporarily. – 3 – delivered to 1st Battery 684 A 228 AX.	G.C.T.

Army Form C. 2118.

WAR DIARY
or
INTELLIGENCE SUMMARY.

(Erase heading not required.)

Instructions regarding War Diaries and Intelligence Summaries are contained in F.S. Regs., Part II. and the Staff Manual respectively. Title pages will be prepared in manuscript.

Hour, Date, Place	Summary of Events and Information	Remarks and references to Appendices
BRONFAY FARM. L.4.c. 14-12-16.	8 D.A.C. Nº 1 Section delivered to 33rd Rgt 912.A 304 AX - 2 Section " " 32nd " 912.A 304 AX - 3 Section " " 8th " 684 A 228 AX	G.C.T.
15-12-16.	Nº 1 Section " " 5th 1st 304 A 456 AX - 2 Section " " 3rd " 684 A 228 AX - 3 Section " " 36th " 684 A 228 AX	G.C.T.
16-12-16.	Nº 1 Section " " 32 & 33rd " 673 A 646 AX Nº 2 " " " 1st & 3rd " 800 A 264 AX Nº 3 " " " 36 & 5th " 456 A 304 AX	G.C.T.
17-12-16.	Nº 1 Section used from Camp 10s to L 4a Nº 1 Section } To 55th & 57th Batteries 1188 BX Nº 2 " Nº 3 "	G.C.T.
18th-12-16.	Nº 1 Section } To 55th & 57th Batteries 1188 BX 2/LT T.S. DOBREE RFA - 2 " joined from England. - 3 " M/a. The driver who went up to MAUREPAS HALTE by train B.Brown. pan Plac. L/Cpl. A. PALMER & 14 R. sent up to Bris. for dump 2 Wagons daily sent up to DADDI's Dir for fatigues from 1 Section 5 Wagons daily sent to R.E. Mericourt for fatigues from 2 & 3 sect.	G.C.T.
23-12-16.	1000 AX 350 BX sent up from PLATEAU to Dump at MAUREPAS	G.C.T.
24-12-16.	500 AX 300 BX sent up from PLATEAU to Dump at MAUREPAS.	G.C.T.

WAR DIARY or INTELLIGENCE SUMMARY

Army Form C. 2118.

(Erase heading not required.)

Hour, Date, Place	Summary of Events and Information	Remarks and references to Appendices
BRONFAY FARM 26.12.16	8 D.A.C. 1000 AX sent up to dump at MAUREPAS from PLATEAU. LTC MILLER RFA D 2/LT —'S DUBREE RFA posted to 45th Bde RFA	G.C.T.
28.12.16	600 AX sent up to MAUREPAS DUMP. 2/LT TS BURRIDGE joined attached from 13th Reserve Regt. f Cavalry. 600 AX sent up to MAUREPAS DUMP	G.C.T.
29.12.16	Orders received re 2 Section going forward being part of 4 H.A. Group. As a result it has to march out full with 76 Rds per gun 18pr. & 48 Rds per gun 4.5" Howitzer. To enable them to complete with rounds 2 Section was posted to them (2 waggons, 136 rounds 8 drivers) 9 additional waggons, complete with spare horses / ditches / spare fillers, 2 gunners)	G.C.T.
30.12.16	Ammunition & Carls. Cape Packs. OB 1B Echelon G.S. wagons for gun teams. (5 GS wagons to carry 27 rds per gun were devolved to march with to carry 66 rds per gun for 4.5" Howitzers 16Pdr gun 24 GS wagons 600 AX sent up to MAUREPAS DUMP. 396 BX sent up to 5th Battery. Following Officers joined from Base :— 2/Lt W.E. Taylor RFA (T.F.), 2/W E.W. Tait RFA (T.F.), 2/Lt M.E. A. Jenden RFA. (T.F.), 2/W E.G. Marsh RFA (S.R) (L. W. W. Murray R.F.A. (T.F.)	G.C.T.
30/31 12/16	No 2 Section to proceed to B Echelon. Wheeles with Ammunition at PLATEAU.	

CONFIDENTIAL.

8th. DIVISIONAL ARTILLERY

WAR DIARY

OF

8. Dvn. Am Col.

From 1.1.17   To 31.1.17

(VOLUME 27)

With Appendices Nos. None

Army Form C. 2118.

WAR DIARY
or
INTELLIGENCE SUMMARY.

(Erase heading not required.)

Instructions regarding War Diaries and Intelligence Summaries are contained in F.S. Regs., Part II. and the Staff Manual respectively. Title pages will be prepared in manuscript.

Hour, Date, Place	Summary of Events and Information	Remarks and references to Appendices
BRAUFAY FARM January 1917.	S.D.A.C. Volume 26.	
1st	600 AX sent up to Dump from Plateau.	Q.C.T.
2nd	600 AX " " " " " "	
	B 2 Echelon G.S. A.A. Section arrived to join Column. Part occupied lines previously occupied by 2 Sections. The rest took over from our No 2 Section 4 D.A.C. Forward Grenade Dump under Lt. FRITH established at COMBLES.	
	About 30,000 Grenades of all kinds sent up to Heis Dump. During next 5 Days, 960,000 S.A.A. drawn to fill up S.A.A. Section Dump at MAUREPAS	
3rd	600 AX 300 BX sent up to Dump at MAUREPAS	Q.C.T.
4th	600 AX 300 BX " " " " " "	Q.C.T.
5th	600 AX 300 BX " " " " " "	Q.C.T.
6th	600 AX 300 BX " " " " " "	Q.C.T.
7th	600 AX 300 BX " " " " " "	Q.C.T.
8th	600 AX 300 BX " " " " " "	Q.C.T.
9th	Orders received for S.A.A. Section (43 G.S. Wagons, 15 S.A.A. carts) to with draw to Back area. 5 G.S. Wagons with Drivers from R.E. Work at Maricourt.	Q.C.T.
10th	300 A. 150 BX sent up to Maurepas B 2 Echelon (S.A.A. Section) marched to BRONFAY, billeting at VAUX. ARGOUVRES on the way. Orders received re reorganisation of Div. Art.	Q.C.T.

WAR DIARY or INTELLIGENCE SUMMARY

Army Form C. 2118.

Hour, Date, Place	Summary of Events and Information	Remarks and references to Appendices
BRONFAY FARM JANUARY 10th	8 D.A.C.	
	New organisation of DAC as under:— A Echelon to consist of 2 Sections only. No 3 reconstituted No 1, and No 2 with following strengths:—	
	A Echelon 4 Officers 2180 R. 22 R. 250 L.D.	
	G.S. wagons whole echelon 23 S.A.A. carts 15.	
	Q.F. wagons 18 pr 36	
	" 4.5" 12.	
	B Echelon Same establishment as 3 G.S. wagons for gun amm'n —	
	No 1 Section down wireless 7 Army Field Artillery B'de Amm'n Column being at present without Howitzer subsection, & carrying No 5 AA amm'n.	
11.30 A.M.	150 B* to Maricourt	
7 pm	Following Officers joined the Column from Base	
	2/Lt E.A. JONES R.F.A. T.F.	Q.C.T.
	2/Lt MORGAN MORGAN R.F.A.—	
	2/Lt H.M. JONES R.F.A. T.F.	
	2/Lt E. FAUNCE DE LAUNE East Kent Yeomanry to 33rd B'de R.F.A.	Q.C.T.
11 pm	2/Lt G FAUNCE DE LAUNE posted	
12 pm	Operation Order No 40 received — New No 1 Section & 5th B'de A.C. to come under orders of 40th Div	Q.C.T.
	affected all echelons. No 1 Section to come under orders of 5th B'de A.C. to come under orders of	Q.C.T.
	Arty from 2 p.m 13th. No. —	
	O.C. 5th B'de RFA from 8 a.m 13th — HQ DAC march to	
13th	ARGOEUVRES on way to Back Area.	Q.C.T.

WAR DIARY
or
INTELLIGENCE SUMMARY.

Army Form C. 2118.

Place	Date	Hour	Summary of Events and Information	Remarks and references to Appendices
			8 D.A.C.	
ARGOEUVRES	14th	8 a.m.	H.Q. DAC marched to DROMESNIL, arriving about 3.30 p.m. Col. F.W. Boteler R.F.A. returned from leave & took over command of the Column, which at present only consists of H.Q. & B Echelon. H.Q. R.A at SELINCOURT.	G.C.T.
	15th		B Echelon sent party of 50 O.R. to 33rd B.D.E.	G.C.T.
	16th		B " sent 100 mules & 8 L.D to 33 B.D. B are to be filled up with remounts, when they come, recovering their own animals & handing over remounts on arrival in present area. Orders received for B Echelon to march under orders of 25th Inf Brigade on 22nd inst.	G.C.T.
	17th		2/Lt W. Rowe RFA posted to D.A.C from 5th Battery R.F.A. Capt R.M.L Hunter RFA, 2/Lt T.P. Bishop RFA, 2/Lt S.G. Rowe RFA struck off the strength on No 1 Section becoming Army Field Artillery B.A.C. Joined from Base – 2/Lt A.F. Stemp RFA – 2/Lt A.O. Ducas RFA – 2/Lt H. Walker RFA – 2/Lt AJ MACK RFA.	G.C.T.
	22nd		H.Q & Div B H.Q.R.A moved up to middle areas. H.Q.D.A.C. and B Echelon left ov DROMESNIL – Communication except by wire difficult. Relieved by 48th Div. WRT AU MONT.	G.C.T.

Army Form C. 2118.

WAR DIARY
or
INTELLIGENCE SUMMARY.
(Erase heading not required.)

Instructions regarding War Diaries and Intelligence Summaries are contained in F. S. Regs., Part II. and the Staff Manual respectively. Title pages will be prepared in manuscript.

Place	Date	Hour	Summary of Events and Information	Remarks and references to Appendices
			8 D.A.C.	
BROMESNIL	28th		Orders received for H.Q. and B Echelon to move up to relieve 40 DAC on 1st inst. - 98 miles	
	30th		7LD relieved from 33rd Bde. on night of 29th inst. — DAC marched to ARGOEUVRES starting at 8 a.m. Roads very bad owing to continued hard frost. B Echelon took 13 hours to cover 24 miles, arriving Argoeuvres at 8 p.m.	G.C.T.
ARGOEUVRES	31st		H.Q. & B Echelon marched to Camp 117. Accommodation ample, but very cold, as only large huts available. Roads still very bad.	G.C.T.

J.M. Stoter [?] Colonel
Comdg 8 DAC

CONFIDENTIAL.

8th DIVISIONAL ARTILLERY.

WAR DIARY

OF

8th Divn. Am Col.

From 1.2.17 To 28.2.17

(VOLUME XXXIII.)

With APPENDICES Nos.

WAR DIARY
or
INTELLIGENCE SUMMARY.
(Erase heading not required.)

Army Form C. 2118.

8 D.A.C.   Volume 27.

Place	Date	Hour	Summary of Events and Information	Remarks and references to Appendices
Camp 117	1/7		Advance party sent forward to take over from S.A.A. section 40 D.A.C. B Echelon moved in at 3 p.m. to L.R.D. 19 sharing lines with B Echelon 40 D.A.C.	G.T.
BRAY	2/7		B Echelon 40 D.A.C. reached our - 8 D.A.C. responsible for supply from W.R.H. HQ D.A.C. at L.10.a.	G.T.
	3/7		No section delivered 960 AX at A.R.P. B.19.b.6.6	R.H.
	4/7		960 AX sent up to A.R.P.	R.H.
	5/7		404 A. 1000 AX. 700 BX sent up to A.R.P. 6 No. 8 A.C. supplied to 83rd Bde R.F.A. 14 No. 8 A.C. supplied to 45 Bde R.F.A. 1 pr L.F. STEMP R.F.A. posted to 1pr Sec from B Echelon	R.H. R.H. R.H.
	6/7		472 AX. 500 BX sent up to A.R.P.	R.H.
	8/7		1000 A. 1000 AX. 448 BX sent up to A.R.P.	R.H.
	9/7		50 BX sent up to A.R.P.	R.H.
	10/7		600 A. 1000 AX 600 BX sent up to A.R.P.	R.H.
	11/7		HQ D.A.C. was fired on by German Aeroplane about 9-30 p.m.	R.H.
	12/7		1000 AX sent up to A.R.P.	R.H.

WAR DIARY
or
INTELLIGENCE SUMMARY.
(Erase heading not required.)

Army Form C. 2118.

Place	Date	Hour	Summary of Events and Information	Remarks and references to Appendices
Bray	13/2/15		8 D.A.C.	
			Headquarters and CAA Section relieved by the HQ and CAA Section of DAC at 8 A.M. CAA Section marched out from Bray Camp to Camp No 3. Any reference to BA&B Report to ADMS as condition of animals of this Section was very satisfactory. Draft 73 OR arrived from Base	RL
	15th		B Echelon delivered to SAILLY LAURETTE 2504 Mills Grenades	RL
	17th		B Echelon delivered to Aisne Dump 9000 Mills 3000 Rifle Grenades	RL
	18th	10.10	B Echelon delivered to AISNE DUMP 2000 Rifle grenade, 1280 998 3" Trench Mortar bombs	RL
	20th		B Echelon delivered 300 2" TM bombs to ABERDEEN 500 3" AISNE DUMP	RL
	26th		Fifteen GS wagons and 100 pack animals & officers and 200 OR of B Echelon moved from Camp 3 to MAUREPAS RAVINE G.19.c.36 and employed in carrying material and ammunition to front line 2nd Lt F.F. STREET wounded	RL

M. Schuster John
Comm'g 8th DAC

Vol 28

CONFIDENTIAL.

8th DIVISIONAL ARTILLERY.

WAR DIARY

OF

8th Divn Am. Col.

From 1.3.17 To 31.3.17

(VOLUME XXIX)

With Appendices Nos. ——

Army Form C. 2118.

WAR DIARY
or
INTELLIGENCE SUMMARY.
(Erase heading not required.)

VOLUME 2

Place	Date	Hour	Summary of Events and Information	Remarks and references to Appendices
			8 D.A.C.	
BRAY.	MARCH 2nd		80 mules, 85 G.S. wagons returned to B Echelon from MAUREPAS RAVINE	G.C.T.
			4th D.A.C. handed over 11,856 Mills, 204 very lights 1", 1196 very 1½", 1680 Grenades No. 20, 270 Stokes 3", 228 P. Grenades, 100 red Cartridges	G.C.T.
	4th		All grenades etc. taken over from 4th D.A.C. sent up to RISNE DUMP. Successful attack by 8 Div on FRITZ trench at ? ? approaches. 2 N.C.O.'s & 8 men sent up to relieve personnel of 4th D.A.C. at Dump in MAUREPAS RAVINE.	G.C.T.
	5th			G.C.T.
	6th		2/Lt. GAIR R.F.A. took over 4th D.A. Dump 2/Lt. E.A. STOCKEM R.F.A. joined from Base	G.C.T.
	7th		2/Lt. GAIR took over A.R.P. from 40th D.A. B Echelon sent up 700 A. to A.R.P.	G.C.T.
	8th		8th D.A. took over command from 40th D.A. No. 1 Section returned to 8 D.A.C. from RAVINE. Attachment to 40th D.A.C.	G.C.T.
	9th		1 Section B Echelon relieved at A.R.P. 400 A - 400 A.X. 200 R.X.	G.C.T.
	11th		2 Section returned to 8 D.A.C. after attachment to 33rd D.A.C.	G.C.T.
	12th		Orders received re new Salvage Scheme. 2 wagons (complete turnout) allotted to D.A.C. for Salvage. 1 other wagon allotted to each of 33rd & 45th Bdes.	G.C.T.
	13th		6 G.S. wagons for C.R.S. 2 2 for Ordnance Officer Canteen work sent to Camp 23 under an Officer for daily fatigue work.	G.C.T.

WAR DIARY or INTELLIGENCE SUMMARY

Army Form C. 2118.

Place	Date	Hour	Summary of Events and Information	Remarks and references to Appendices
BRAY	14-3-17		8 DAC. 28 GS wagons reporting daily to Bords office XV Corps av Querrieu. 1 wagon to Corp Commander Etinehen	O.C.T.
	16-3-17		Following Officer joined the Bde. 2/Lt W.H. Milford R.F.A. 2/Lt P.S. Smith 2/Lt F.G. Sawyer R.F.A	O.C.T.
	18-3-17		36th Battery & minus 55th Battery moved forward to support advance of infantry on retiring of the Germans.	O.C.T.
	21-3-17		8 GS wagons had 1 section and 7 wagons from 2 section sent forward to billets to Corps.	
			10 wagons from B Echelon to Corps p.163 for same work & road.	O.C.T.
	24-3-17		Proceeded to 2 section sent forward to Clery where 2/Lt Stockin R.F.A. to join pts At Mobile	
			Column to supply 36th Battery & one section of 55th Battery, consisting of 6 wagons Q.F. 18 P², 2 wagons Q.F. 4.5 Howitzer and 2 G.S. wagons.	
			Joined from Base 2/Lt A.H.B. Bower R.F.A. 2/Lt D.L. Roberts R.F.A. 2/Lt M.S. Forness R.F.A	O.C.T.
	26-3-17 27-3-17		2/Lt. G.A. Button R.F.A. 22 L.D. Drawn from CERISY. D.A.C. moved to ALLAINES 14.6.5.8. All sections had to send teams back same night, as	
			owing to shortage of wagons & horses they were unable to move all their stores.	
			2/Lt W.H. Milford R.F.A 2/Lt Forness R.F.A. sent to Corps in T.M.B with 12 men	O.C.T.
	28-3-17		B Echelon handed over 1,383,000 S.A.A to O.S.A. D.A.C. sent to fetch 136 L.D. remounts from	

Army Form C. 2118.

WAR DIARY
or
INTELLIGENCE SUMMARY.
(Erase heading not required.)

8 D.A.C.

Place	Date	Hour	Summary of Events and Information	Remarks and references to Appendices
ALLAINES	28-3-17		CERISY. 2/Lt GAIR R.F.A. & party from A.R.P. collected by wagons B Echelon on night of 27th. 3 pending night in old D.A.C. Camp. Arrived here at 7 p.m. 28th inst.	G.C.T.
	29-3-17		B Echelon Salved from BOUCHAVESNES 353 Boxes Mills. 280 Boxes Stokes 3" 260 Boxes Rifle Grenades No 23, Delivered to 23rd Infantry Bde dump MOISLAINS.	
			2/Lt GAIR R.F.A. formed new A.R.P. in ruins at entrance to MOISLAINS.	G.C.T.
	30-3-17		D.A.C. Salved A 1545 AX 1201 from Battery Dumps & Delivered to A.R.P. Lt W.H DON sent on to form new grenade dump next to A.R.P. BEtween Guo Boro Mills & Delivered & Infantry dump. Joined from Base Lt Eggleton & 2/Lt J.D.COLES R.F.A.	G.C.T.
	31-3-17		Salved & Delivered to A.R.P. A 1392 AX 964 BX 576 RX " " " SAA dump Stokes 3" 513 rounds Mills 3600 Rifle No 23. 888.	G.C.T.
			2/Lt F.E FR.T.A R.F.A. (sick) 2/Lt E.F. STREET R.F.A (wounded) Struck off strength with effect from 15-3-17.	

CONFIDENTIAL.

8th DIVISIONAL ARTILLERY.

WAR DIARY

OF

8th Divn Am Column

From 1.4.17 To 30.4.17

(VOLUME 30)

With Appendices Nos. ....

WAR DIARY
or
INTELLIGENCE SUMMARY.
(Erase heading not required.)

Army Form C. 2118.

VOLUME 29.

Place	Date	Hour	Summary of Events and Information	Remarks and references to Appendices
ALLAINES	1-4-17		8 D.A.C.	
			Following Posting to Brigade	
			33rd Bde R.F.A. Lt R. EGGLETON R.F.A. 45th Bde R.F.A. 2/Lt F.G. SAWYER R.F.A.	
			W.A. MILLIGAN - - D.L. ROBERTS -	
			2/Lt F. SAWYER - - M.S. FURNESS -	
			- P.S. SMITH - - A.G. BUTTON -	
			- J.D. COLES -	
			Salved from Battery positions in Back Area sent to A.R.P.	
			2,128.A 418 AX. Salved sent to Grenade Dump 46 Boxes Mills. 22 Boxes Stokes. 22 Boxes Grenades No 23. 337 Boxes S.A.A.	QCT
	2-4-17		Salved sent to A.R.P. 1,736.A 507 AX. Ten wagon loads of grenades S.A.A. Salved	QCT
	3-4-17		" " " " 1,235.A 665 AX. 4 " " " "	QCT
	4-4-17		" " " " 1,397.A 490 AX. 5 " " " "	QCT
	5-4-17		" " " " 469 BX. Advanced A.R.P. formed at NURLU	QCT
	7-4-17		" " " " 1,034 BX. " Grenade Dump formed at NURLU	QCT
			In view of the amount of work being done Ecoust[?] wagons to cease running. Ammunition from back area to be collected in future & Dumped in side of weaker long road for subsequent collection.	QCT

Army Form C. 2118.

WAR DIARY
or
INTELLIGENCE SUMMARY.
(Erase heading not required.)

Place	Date	Hour	Summary of Events and Information	Remarks and references to Appendices
			& BAC VOLUME 29	
ALLAINES	8-4-17		Collected & Dumped at B.12.6.1.1. 1730 BX, at C.1.C.8.6 170A 181 AX	Q.C.T.
	9-4-17		R Echelon started to collect general etc Dumped on MOISLAINS - BOUCHAVESNES Road. Now open Eight wagon loads per day to be sent & Delivered at MORLU	
	10-4-17		Collected & Dumped at B.17.6.3.6. 1824A & AX	Q.C.T.
			456 BX collected from 57th Battery position Delivered to A.R.P.	Q.C.T.
	11-4-17		587 AB 403 AX salved & Dumped at C.1.D.00. 1104 BX salved & Delivered to A.R.P.	Q.C.T.
	12-4-17		390 BX salved from 63rd Battery position & stacked on roadside C.20.C.8.8. Two both our & however as it had to be moved for 2 miles on hollies. 288 BX sent to A.R.P. from 57th Bg position	C.C.T.
	13-4-17		105 BX Stacked at C.20.C.8.8. 240 BX sent to A.R.P.	Q.C.T.
	14-4-17		1115 AB 147 AX salved & stacked at C.7.9.7.7. 96 BX delivered to A.R.P.	Q.C.T.
	17-4-17		New railhead opened at QUINCONCE about 1.15 central. 892 BX sent up from New head to A.R.P.	C.C.T.
			384 BX sent up to 55th Battery from A.R.P. (Gun position)	C.C.T.
	18-4-17		384 BX sent up to 55th gun line. 378 A 456 AX sent up to Battery Wagon lines	Q.C.T.
			350 AX to 41st R.F.A Division	Q.C.T.
	19-4-17		In view of fact that owing to shortage of horses both AE B Echelons were immobile. It was decided to make A Echelon at least mobile. In consequence of this the	Q.C.T.

WAR DIARY or INTELLIGENCE SUMMARY

Army Form C. 2118.

Place	Date	Hour	Summary of Events and Information	Remarks and references to Appendices
ALLAINES	19.4.17	8 a.m.	Column was reorganized as Echelon coupled with complement of S.A.A vehicles, while B Echelon took over vehicles for reserve of Corps Gun Ammunition. After the transfer of Animals B Echelon only had 15 riders 2 drivers D & 16 mules left. All troop references left as (Map 62c) 110 L.D. were also sent. 60 to 33rd DSD to 41st Bde as remounts	G.T.
V.26.c.	20.4.17		As DAC was considered to be too far back owing to A.R.P. having been moved forward to NURLU, it was moved to Riverside Wood about V.26.c central (57c) HQ occupied an old German gun position. Move completed by midday.	G.T.
	21.4.17		Further reorganisation of convoys of SAA etc carried — 15 SAA carts sent as complete turn out to be attached 5 to each Infantry Brigade. Of the 12 GS wagons in A Echelon now Three are in future to carry 210 rounds Stokes Mortar Ammn: 3" & 6 light Trench Mortars each, while 3 of the 10 wagons for SAA in B Echelon carries 240 rounds Stokes 3" each. 1 Section now has 8 GS wagons for SAA 320,000 2 wagons for grenades (2760) & 1 wagon for Stokes (210). 2 Section has 7 wagons for SAA (280,000) 2 wagons for Stokes (420) 1 wagon for Grenades (1380). B Echelon has 17 GS wagons for SAA (680,000) & GS wagons for Stokes (720) &	

Army Form C. 2118.

WAR DIARY
or
INTELLIGENCE SUMMARY.
(Erase heading not required.)

Place	Date	Hour	Summary of Events and Information	Remarks and references to Appendices
K.26.C. (57c)	21-4-17		8.D.A.C.	
			1 wagon for grenades (1380). Total S.A.A. & grenades etc was carried in D.A.C. 10 S.A.A. 1,280,000. Mills grenades 5520. Stokes 3" 1350. When Division 10 Stationary all establishment of S.A.A and B Echelon is deposited at main Divisional Bomb Depot. This amount is kept up to strength by indent from D.A.C. on Division Q on notification by Officer i/c Divl Dump that any of Deposit has been used.	G.C.T.
	22-4-17		About 30 wagon loads of gun ammunition were sent up daily for three days to Batteries wagon lines from A.R.P.	G.C.T.
	24-4-17			
	25-4-17		New scheme of Ammn supply started – On receipt of wire by 3pm daily D.A.C. supplies not more than 16 wagon loads to each Brigade & delivers to gun positions. In addition to this ammunition if required has to be sent to 33rd Bde wagon lines at SOREL.	G.C.T.
	26-4-17		12 wagon loads of B.X. to 55th Battery gun line. 38 wagon loads of B.X. & 18pr sent up to gun positions	G.C.T.
	27-4-17		6 wagon loads of 18pr to 3rd Battery gun positions	G.C.T.
	28-4-17		26 wagon loads of 18pr to gun positions	G.C.T.

WAR DIARY or INTELLIGENCE SUMMARY

Army Form C. 2118.

Place	Date	Hour	Summary of Events and Information	Remarks and references to Appendices
V.26.C.	28.4.17		8 D.A.C. 75 Heavy T.M. 9.45" Bombs drawn from Clery & delivered to A.D.P., & thence to Battery position. Wagon left A.D.P. at 10 p.m. & did not get back till 6 a.m. 29th owing to authorised load of 15 bombs being too much for 3t wagon across country.	G.T.
	29.4.17		29 wagon loads of stores sent up to gun positions. With a view to following operations an advanced dump of gun ammunition was formed on right hand side of main (long road) from FINS - HEUDECOURT about W.7.C.2.2. Ground absolutely open, & camouflage the only way of screening dump, which was established 50 yards apart. Two single dumps to consist of more than 3000 rounds. During the month owing to the increasing wastage of horses & Divisional Artillery not staying for hours was established at ALLAINES, so by sending horses to M.V.S. they were lost to the artillery. Two remounts were available. 3 shelters supplied a fair no. of N.C.Os to assist in this. During the month by means of pushing forward patrols Direct attacks on villages VV. & Division took COURCELCOURT on 19th, VILLERS GUISLAINS out & GONNELIEU on 21st April.	G.T. G.T. G.T.

J.M.D. Fitzpatrick
Capt. D.A.C.

CONFIDENTIAL.

8th DIVISIONAL ARTILLERY.

WAR DIARY
OF
8' Div'n Am Column

From 1.5.17 To 31.5.17

(VOLUME XXXI)

With Appendices Nos. —

Vol 30

WAR DIARY
or
INTELLIGENCE SUMMARY.
(Erase heading not required.)

Army Form C. 2118.

VOLUME 3ɸ.

& D.A.C.

Place	Date	Hour	Summary of Events and Information	Remarks and references to Appendices
V 263	May 1-5-17		Drawn from A.R.P. Sent to Gun lines 45th Bde AX 436 BX 144. 33rd Bde AX456 BX 288	G.C.T.
(N° NURLU)	2-5-17		" " " " " 45th " — AX 988 33rd " — AX 632 BX 192	G.C.T.
	3-5-17		" " " " " 45th " AX 912 BX. 192 33rd " — BX 192 A912	G.C.T.
	4-5-17		" " " " " 45th " AX 1140 BX. 192 A.76 35th " — AX — BX 368 A912	G.C.T.
	5-5-17		" " " " " 45th " AX 456 BX 192 A.456 33rd " — BX 192 A 48	G.C.T.
	6-5-17		" " " " " 45th " AX 304 BX 192 33rd " — M.1	G.C.T.
	7-5-17		Main Divisional Bomb Depot moved from D.9 to W 146 close to HEUDICOURT.	G.C.T.
	8-5-17		228 AX & 192 BX sent up to 45th Bde. 192 BX sent up to 33rd Bde.	G.C.T.
	10-5-17		Drawn from A.R.P & sent to Gun lines 45th Bde A.228	R.R.
	12-5-17		" " " " " 33rd " A.399 AX.133 BX 384	R.R.
	13-5-17		N° 1 & 2 Sec S.delived from back area A.64f AX228 delivered to A.R.P	R.R.
	14-5-17		A.1335 AX.1857 BX612	
	15-5-17		40 Ker relieved foll Gun in line between 12th & 13th May. N° 1 & 2 Sec S Cnrad from	R.R.
	16-5-17		HEUDECOURT DUMP & A.R.P NURLU A.704 BX.668.	R.R.
	17.5.17		N° 1 & 2 Sec S delived from back area A.1071 A.145 BPC Sec S delivered A.R.P A.1436 AX624 BX 460 "	R.R.

Army Form C. 2118.

WAR DIARY
or
INTELLIGENCE SUMMARY.
(Erase heading not required.)

8th D.A.C.

Place	Date	Hour	Summary of Events and Information	Remarks and references to Appendices
	May			
V.26.C.	16th		A Echelon filled up to establishment	R.H.
"	20th		D.A.C. moved from RIVERSIDE WOOD to CAMP III. B Echelon were supplied	R.H.
			B Echelon and 8th H.Q. to assist in the move from 8.45 Coy Ord Train & to convoy	
			B Echelon received 132 L.D. 72 Cordite mules	
Camp III	21st		B Echelon filled to establishment at HEILLY Less 4 wagons lent to	M.H.
			move T.M.C. (160,000 rounds S.A.A)	
	22nd		D.A.C. commenced entraining at HEILLY and EDGEHILL keeping	R.H.
			divided into 13 trains	
RENESCURE 23rd			to move completed D.A.C. arrived at RENESCURE and were	R.H.
			received in excellent billets	
	25th		Received order to move from RENESCURE to CLAIR MARAIS	R.H.
			D.A.C. moved to CLAIR MARAIS M.22.A.8.1.	
CLAIR MARAIS	26th		He column commenced their annual training	R.H.
"	27th			R.H.
"	28th		Draft of 18 men joined T.M.C. and proceeded to POPERINGHE	R.H.
"	30th		9th M.H. and 2th R.O.A.H. joined from Base. D.A.C. drew 265 Tanks from ARQUES	R.H.
			and delivered 138 at RENESCURE refilled 85 delivered 132 at WARDRECQUES.	
			and filled 125 for Guards Div	

Army Form C. 2118.

WAR DIARY
or
INTELLIGENCE SUMMARY.
(Erase heading not required.)

Instructions regarding War Diaries and Intelligence Summaries are contained in F.S. Regs., Part II. and the Staff Manual respectively. Title pages will be prepared in manuscript.

Place	Date	Hour	Summary of Events and Information	Remarks and references to Appendices
CLAIRMARAIS	May 31st		8th D.A.C.	R.L.
			D.A.C. generals commenced training with 33rd and 45th Bdes R.F.A.	

J.M. Slater ? Mnel
(Comd) 8 D.A.C.

CONFIDENTIAL.

Vol 31

8th DIVISIONAL ARTILLERY.

WAR DIARY
OF
8th Div. A.M. Column

From 1st June '17 To 30th June 1917

(VOLUME XXXII)

With Appendices Nos.

Army Form C. 2118.

WAR DIARY
or
INTELLIGENCE SUMMARY.
(Erase heading not required.)

VOLUME 31

Instructions regarding War Diaries and Intelligence Summaries are contained in F.S. Regs., Part II. and the Staff Manual respectively. Title pages will be prepared in manuscript.

Place	Date	Hour	Summary of Events and Information	Remarks and references to Appendices
	JUNE		& DAC	
CLAIRMARAIS	4-6-17		G.O.C. R.A. 8th Divn. inspected the Column in full marching order. G.O.C. 8 Divn. came later in time to see the last section.	G.C.T.
	6-6-17		2/Lt N. HORGAN-GAUL R.F.A. - 2/Lt G.R.P. BROWN R.F.A. and 2/Lt C.H. HASKINS R.F.A. joined from Base. 2/Lt B.H. ROACH R.F.A. posted to 33 B.D.S., 2/Lt O.V.R.H.B. HILL R.F.A. posted to 45th Bde.	Q.C.T.
	6-6-17		2/Lt E.V. MORGAN R.F.A. to 7 Divn: Lt W.H. DON R.F.A. rejoined from 4th Army Gunnery School	Q.C.T.
	7-6-17		Preliminary heats held for Divn: Sport run off as usual & entries for Column races (mules)	Q.C.T.
	8-6-17		1 Officer & 50 men sent to CALAIS to draw remounts for 10th Corps.	Q.C.T.
	9-6-17		25 O.R. sent to CALAIS to draw remounts for 8th Divl. M.G. Divisional Sports. B Echelon won the Challenge Cup for best aggregate of marks for team events. 2/Lt A.G. LUCAS R.F.A. to hospital.	Q.C.T.
	12-6-17		No 1 Section @ proprietor of B Echelon marched to CAESTRE area at 15 hours notice, starting at 11 a.m. Route ARQUES - FORT ROUGE - LONGUE CROIX - LE PEUPLIER CAESTRE Area being full they were diverted to BORRE, & did not get into billet till 9 p.m. All the time DAC was in rest & training area, Gunners went to Gun drill daily with Brigades, & a signalling class under 2/Lt T. GAIR R.F.A. was held at D.H.E.	G.C.T.
	13-6-17		H.Q., 2 Section & remainder of B Echelon marched to CAESTRE area at 10.30 a.m. Route	

WAR DIARY
or
INTELLIGENCE SUMMARY.

Army Form C. 2118.

Place	Date	Hour	Summary of Events and Information	Remarks and references to Appendices
	13-6-17		S.D.A.C. HAUT SCHOURROUF (Sheet 27) thence by same route to join Coly of Column Billets in HONDEGHEM (H.Q & B Echelon). N° 2 Section at LA BREARDE	G.C.T.
CAESTRE Crea	13-6-17 6-17		N° 1 Section & proportion of B Echelon marched on to camps near POPERINGHE at G.14.b.1.8 (Sheet 28), arriving in billets about 5.30 p.m.	G.C.T.
	14-6-17		H.Q. 2 Section & remainder of B Echelon moved at 7 a.m. to camps in POPERINGHE area, arriving at 1.30 p.m. (Map Sheet 28)	
			Disposition. H.Q. G.20.G.31 — 1 Section G.14.b.18 — 2 Section G.15.c.55 — B Echelon G.14.d.55	
			H.Q. Div. and R.A. at H.Q. central. Section had camps with lines, which they took over. H.Q. D.A.C. had no billets, but managed to knock up tents & shelters from AREA Commandant. Ammunition Dumps in charge of LT. P.B. NUNN R.F.A. at H.14.b.5.8 & G.16.d. S.A.A. Dump in charge N.2/Lt. Leach at H.16.D.11. (Sheet 28)	G.C.T.
	15-6-17 ↓		18. Q.F. Wagon 18-P.d.B. Q.F. with howitzers set up to 4th B. in 115.G. One got ditched & fairs to get there. Remainder got back at 2.30 a.m. after starting at 11 p.m.	G.C.T.
	16-6-17		2/Lt. Dor. R.F.A. set up to reconnoitre two additional Dumps at School I.9.C. Sat T.15.c. Order received to empty Dump at G.16.d at once, it being required for Heavy M R.P. Impossible to finish in one day as no lorries turned up. 5000 B.S. sent up on [illegible] this first day.	
			2/Lt. G.R.P. BROWN R.F.A. posted to W/E Train from Battery.	

WAR DIARY
or
INTELLIGENCE SUMMARY.
(Erase heading not required.)

Army Form C. 2118.

Place	Date	Hour	Summary of Events and Information	Remarks and references to Appendices
8 D.A.C.	17/6/17		Daily fatigue of 4 G.S. wagons at 3am @ 11am to load timber from KRUUSTRAAT to ZILLEBEKE, working 8 hours per ship.	
	18/6/17		Dump at G.16.D emptied by help of lorries, & whole party were ordered to main dump at H.16.6.5.6. 5 G.S. wagon loads of S.A.A. etc sent up from S.A.A. Dump at H.16.D.11 to Gordon house dump at T.16.D.S.8. Traffic blocked road & loads were dumped at I.22.c. 2 wagons sent to move light T.M. Battery for 24th Infty Bde. Cut owing to Guides being sent lost their way.	4 CT
	19/6/17		5 G.S. wagons with S.A.A. etc had same experience @ had to dump loads close to the & previous night. Heavy shelling @ cmd road was blocked by two way traffic then being no room to pass. 1 Mule injured & had to be shot. Wiring party of 50 men from R.M.E. to bury cable to be sent up for Bethune night. 1 Man wounded that night. 4 8 G.S. wagon loads of R.E. material down from R.E. yard @ rear to B'n wagon lines.	4 CT
	20/6/17		Third attempt to get S.A.A. & fire etc to 1/16 D (Scottish Dump) Infantry Guide to be sent to show the way.	4 CT

Army Form C. 2118.

WAR DIARY
or
INTELLIGENCE SUMMARY.
(Erase heading not required.)

Instructions regarding War Diaries and Intelligence Summaries are contained in F. S. Regs., Part II. and the Staff Manual respectively. Title pages will be prepared in manuscript.

Place	Date	Hour	Summary of Events and Information	Remarks and references to Appendices
			8 D.A.C.	
Poperinghe Area	20th		Lieut W.H. Don R.F.A. posted to 45 B? 2/Lt. A.G. Lucas RFA rejoined from hospital	Q.C.T.
	21st		S.A.A. load of SAA etc successfully delivered at Gordon House dump. 1 Mule injured & destroyed. 1 Man wounded. 2/Lt N. Morgan eau? RFA 2/Lt C.H. Hakins RFA posted to 33 B? RFA also 35 Gunners & 6 drivers.	Q.C.T.
			10 wagon loads of SAA etc received from Warrington road by night.	
	23rd		Fatigue party of 1 Officer & 50 OR detailed for work on burying telephone lines every alternate night. 2/Lt A.H. Bolmer R.F.A. 15 Gunners & 9 drivers posted to 45 B?. During night 22/23 1 G.S. wagon sent to take	Q.C.T.
	24th		R.S. material up to gun lines. 1 man wounded 6 horses killed.	Q.C.T.
			5 wagon loads of SAA sent up to Gordon House Dump. 2/Lt Mark Duke R.F.A. joined from Base 1 Mule wounded. Fatigue of 6 G.S. wagons to report at 8 p.m. each night at Pioneer Dump (H.21.6.8.4)	Q.C.T.
	25/17		24 Q.F.18Pr wagons sent to deliver Am. to Y B? positions in T.16.9.16. Only 4 got there owing partly to heavy shelling (1sect) & partly no guides arriving (2sect) 1 man wounded 2 mules killed 5 mules wounded. Our 8 teams which were together in one party there were casualties in 7. (1 sect).	Q.C.T.
	26/9		24 Q.F. 18P? wagon sent up to X B? position near to Y B? position 6 men wounded 6 animals killed 3 wounded 1 wagon badly damaged (1B? section)	Q.C.T.
	27/9		12 18Pr Q.F. wagon & 12 4.5 wagon sent up to Y B? positions Potsdam etc., & w shelling. Handed over Vancouver Dump to 16th D.A. taking over Dump (Granville) at H.13 central from 30 D.A	Q.C.T.

WAR DIARY
or
INTELLIGENCE SUMMARY.
(Erase heading not required.)

Army Form C. 2118.

Place	Date	Hour	Summary of Events and Information	Remarks and references to Appendices
& D.Ac.	27/6/17		VANCOUVER DUMP has been shelled slightly for last two days but on night 26/27 it was heavily shelled, but no damage was done. 2/Lt LEACH RFA established at advanced Div: Bomb Dump at GORDON HOUSE, Copl WEBSTER being left in charge of Main Dump at H.16.d.1.1. 2/Lt. C.E. PROCTOR RFA joined from Base.	G.C.T.
	28/6/17		D.A.C. sent to PROVEN & drew 6 Charges 12 riders 8 6 L.D. for Div: Arty. receiving 1 R. 23 L.D for column. 4 G.S. wagons loads of 2" T.M. Bombs sent up to School I.9.c., also 10 Limbered G.S loads to Gordon House Dump. Casualties. 2 O.R. wounded.	G.C.T.
	29/6/17		12 wagon loads of BX sent up to X Brigade positions. Draft of 89 gunners & 50 Drivers arrived from Base. Casualties NIL.	G.C.T.
	30/6/17		12 wagon loads of 18p? & 12 wagon loads N.4.5 sent up to X Brigade positions by day owing to bad weather & poor visibility. SAA wagons failed to get up owing to lorry being broken down on a bridge. On journey back track was shelled, two Drivers being wounded, 2 animals killed & 1 wounded. Orders received for a [strike] nightly delivery of 10 Limbered G.S loads of S.A.A grenades etc. to Gordon House dump.	G.C.T. G.C.T.

M. Sketer John
Comp 8th D.A.C.

CONFIDENTIAL.

8th DIVISIONAL ARTILLERY.

WAR DIARY

OF

8th D.A. Ammunition Column

From 1.7.17 To 30.7.17

(VOLUME XXXIII)

With APPENDICES Nos. ———

WAR DIARY or INTELLIGENCE SUMMARY

Army Form C. 2118.

8th D.A.C.

VOLUME 32.

Place	Date	Hour	Summary of Events and Information	Remarks and references to Appendices
POPERINGHE AREA	July 1st		Orders received to send up daily from Divn. S.A.A. dump to Gordon House 36,000 S.A.A. 2000 Mills No 5, 2000 Mills No 23, 120 Stokes 3", 150 Green Cartridges. Cable party of 1 Officer, 60 men detailed for 3 weone nights 1/2, 3/4, 5/6. 12 wagon loads B.X. sent up to Y Brigade position – Joindram Barr. 2/LE M Holcroft R.F.A. – H.C. Rosa R.F.A. – E F Bryan R.F.A. – Casualties 1 mule slightly wounded. A.S. Goodall R.F.A. – A.C. Whitehouse R.F.A. All S.R.	G.C.T.
	2nd		12 wagon loads B.X. 9 12 wagon loads 18 pr. sent up to Y & X Brigade respectively, also 10 in load G.S. loads of S.A.A. etc. Traffic very congested. Casualties Nottle heavy 8 Drivers wounded, A? whom remained at duty. 2 animals were killed, 4 missing, 10 wounded.	
	3rd		Trail fatigue altered, & licenced to 10 wagons to report to 3rd Canadian Labour Batte or Pioneer Camp. 2/Lt G.E. Rodin R.F.A. pushes to 3rd Battery R.F.A. 2 gunners & 1 Driver posted to 45 Bde., 2 Drivers to 33 Bde., also 16 gunners to W/8 T.M. Battery	G.C.T.
	4th		6 wagons B.X. 9 12 wagon 18 pr. sent up to 45 Bde position. 576 gunners & 268 B.X. sent up to W. Bde gun position. 3 mules wounded.	G.C.T.
	5th		Cable party continued every alternate day. 912 A&AX 266 B.X. sent up to 45 Bde. 1 Mule wounded. To 232 Bde. 912. 18 pr. & 288 B.X.	G.C.T.
	6th		To 45 Bde. 912 A & AX. 240 B.X. 1 mule killed 4 wounded.	G.C.T.

WAR DIARY or INTELLIGENCE SUMMARY

Army Form C. 2118.

Place	Date	Hour	Summary of Events and Information	Remarks and references to Appendices
8 DAC	6th		To W Brigade been Mixed groups. 1852 ABAX. Arrangement made for un Co deliver 14160 ABAX to the Brigade by 13th inst. There would mean 12 wagon per section each night. 1 Mule killed 2 mules B.I.L.D. wounded.	G.C.T.
	7th		To W Brigade 912 ABAX. Casualties nil. Scheme Willing W. position cancelled, owing to arrival of W 13th DAC now have to turn up ammn as details from H.Q.R.A. Canadian parque. A/C wagons hampered to 25th D.A.C. The parque had been very laborious owing to length of hours @ dump. Dge. to wagons (by carriage of iron rations 2 C.S. wagon @ teams without drew of 6 R.Dns complete with saddles, sent to 1st AFARS, attached SA personnel only 2/Lt A.S. Goodall RFA posted to 36 B.D. 2/Lt M. Duke RFA posted to 6 Div. T.M.	G.C.T.
	8th		To 33 B.Dx R.F.A A776 AY 344 BX 240. Casualties 1 man killed. 3 animals killed 2 wounded. 3 wagons G.S. for 2" @ 6 P.S. for 6" T.M. ammn detailed nightly to take ammn forward. 6 wagon posted on 10th inst.	G.C.T.
	9th		To 33 B.Dx A 636 AX 188. To 45th Bdx BX 576. Casualties 1 man killed 9 men wounded, 4 animals killed 9 wounded. B Echelon having failed to get grenades etc up the previous night sent up a double lot successfully.	G.C.T.
	10th		To 33 B.Dx A 608 AX 228 — 45 B.D. RPS 432. Casualties NIL. All wagons had to be clear of KRUISTRAAT – KRUISTRAAT HOEK line by 11 a.m. because of Artillery operation.	G.C.T.

WAR DIARY
or
INTELLIGENCE SUMMARY

Army Form C. 2118.

8 D.A.C.

Place	Date	Hour	Summary of Events and Information	Remarks and references to Appendices
POPERINGHE	July 11th		To 33 Bde: A110D AX344 BX288. Casualties 1 Mule killed. Cable bringing fatigue completed.	G.C.T.
	12th		To VOID. 516 Strick shell 4.5" How – To 110 Bde – A684 AX 226. Casualties 5 animals wounded. 2/Lt T. GAIR RFA sent up to relieve 2/Lt F. READ RFA at Advanced Grenade dump at Gordon House.	G.C.T.
	13th		2/Lt E.W. TAIT RFA 2/Lt H.C. ROJA RFA @ 20 OR sent on a T.M. course, half hour, half hour at 2nd Army School of Mortars. LEULINGHEM. Course to last 3 weeks. To 33 Bde: A720 AX192. Casualties 5 men wounded, 4 animals killed 89 wounded.	
	14th		141 Remounts drawn from POPERINGHE @ Dickebusch to R.D.s. D.A.C. kept 3R & L.D. 47 mules. To C/VOTE (36B.) A340 AX 116. N°2 Section failed to get through owing to people in front of them unlooking @ leaving wagons on track owing to heavy shelling. Casualties 2 mules killed & 1 wounded.	G.C.T.
	15th		Joined from Base Lt T.A. WILLIAMS RGA @ posted to w/e T.M. Battery. 2/Lt J.E.N. ALBRECHT RFA posted to 2 Section; 2/Lt H.R. LATIMER RFA posted to B Echelon, 2/Lt T.E. WOOD RFA to 1 Section. 2/Lt W. ROWE sent up to relieve 2/Lt T. GAIR at Grenade dump at GORDON HOUSE.	
		3am	SAA dump at 19.16.D.1.1 shelled. Very light etc set on fire, which spread to Stokes. Whole place burned with the exception of train full of Rifle grenades 23 @ Stokes bombs on other side of road. No casualties. N° 96774 D² WHITE (1 section) awarded Military medal for gallantry @	

WAR DIARY
or
INTELLIGENCE SUMMARY.
(Erase heading not required.)

Army Form C. 2118.

Place	Date	Hour	Summary of Events and Information	Remarks and references to Appendices
S.D.A.C.	15th		Devotion to Duty on two occasions in particular, whilst taking Amm'n up to the guns under heavy shell fire.	G.C.T.
			No more Amm'n to be drawn from A.R.P till Battery positions have been cleared. 5000 Rifle grenades No 23, 1000 Stokes 3" Sent up to Goden House. Casualties 2 men wounded @ 3 wides.	G.C.T.
	16th		Joined from BASE Lt J.A. WILLIAMS RGA & posted to W/B T.M. Battery. Posted to DAC 2/Lt T.E.M ALBRECHT RFA, 2/Lt H.R LATIMER RFA. 2/Lt A.E WOOD RFA. 2/Lt W ROWE RFA sent up to relieve 2/Lt T. GAIR RFA at Goden House. GGS wagons sent up with T.M Amm'n CASUALTIES NIL.	G.C.T.
	17th		Owing to increase in Dump at Gwel 1520 A 304AX @ 152 BX sent up to 46 B.dy. 2/Lt T.E.M ALBRECHT RFA posted to 65th Battery. Casualties 6 mules wounded.	G.C.T.
	19th		Owing to Dump at H 16 D11 having been partially destroyed, grenades etc which were saved were moved to new dump at H 23 C 2.1. 2/Lt H.R LATIMER RFA posted to W/B @ 2/Lt A.E WOOD RFA to X/B T.M. Battery. Ac 45774 Dr G.F WHITE awarded Military Medal for Devotion to Duty @ Gallactic, n' YPRES on 25-6-7.	G.C.T.

Army Form C. 2118.

WAR DIARY
or
INTELLIGENCE SUMMARY.
(Erase heading not required.)

Place	Date	Hour	Summary of Events and Information	Remarks and references to Appendices
POPERINGHE	20		8 D.A.C. 2/Lt AC WHITEHOUSE RFA posted to 1st Battery. 15 Gunners posted to 33 Bt.	G.C.T.
	22		No 11157 Sgt. RE Westlake & No 79650 Dvr J. Halliwell awarded Military Medal for Gallantry & devotion to duty while taking up Amm'ts to Gun positions under fire. Fred at H.23 to be allotted to D.A.C. for 2/Lt M. SLADE forward Wagon Lines. Each section of A Echelon to send up 100 pack animals to be at Cal of B Bt. Commander. B Echelon to send up 120 pack mules & 15 Airbourne S.A. Wagons for use of Infantry. 67/6 BX sent up to 55 Battery, 2 men wounded entrained with unit (invalided) 7 wounded. 2 men wounded but remained with section	G.C.T.
	23		2/Lt W P TULLOCH GAR. RFA posted as Signal Officer to 103/Bt RFA. 2/Lt J M SLADE RFA joined from Base. 12 wagon loads of A.A.X delivered to 5G Battery. 1 man wounded gassed No 68024 D'Murphy. 5 wagons sent up to 171 Tunn. Co. to carry stores forward. 2/Lt J M SLADE RFA joined from Base.	G.C.T.
	24		40 pack animals sent up to collect Amm'n in forward area for 55 Battery.	G.C.T.
	25		380.A 114AX to B/ACTOR 288 Gas shell to 55th Battery	G.C.T.
	26		456A to 3rd Battery, 342A 114 AX to 32nd Battery. No 170828 Driver Jones F. wounded 2 animals wounded 40 Pack animals sent up to 55 Battery to collect Amm'n in forward area.	G.C.T.

WAR DIARY or INTELLIGENCE SUMMARY

Army Form C. 2118.

Place	Date	Hour	Summary of Events and Information	Remarks and references to Appendices
Poperinghe Area	26		8 D.A.C. Draft of 158 O.R. from Base, 134 sent out direct to Brigades	G.C.T.
	27		To 52 Battery A646 AX 266. 1 Rider wounded	G.C.T.
	28		To 1st Battery A626 AX 226 To 51 BX 288. 53 L.D. for Brigade @ 24 Mules for DAC. Joined & Collected by DAC. 2/Lt LEACH RFA sent up to relieve 2/Lt ROWE RFA at Gordon House	G.C.T. G.C.T.
	29.		To 33 Bde. A1406 AX 246 BX 286. Casualties NIL	G.C.T.
	30		Y Day 15 Limbered G.S. wagons of B. Echelon sent up in small parties between 3 p.m & 8 p.m. These walked about Belgian Chateau area until dusk & then moved into advanced W.K. at H.23.b, having loaded up with S.A.A. Grenades etc at V. dump. Casualties during month. Personnel 2 Killed 20 wounded all O.R., 1 of whom died of wounds. Animals 16 mules killed by shell fire 6 R. 2 L.D. 60 mules wounded by shell fire of which 28 were sent to M.V.S. Of the O.R. Casualties there were Artillery 15 wounded & Gassed, who remained at duty. Capt C.F. VIVIAN RFA awarded the Military Cross for gallantry & devotion to duty near YPRES during June & early July. 143,757 A. 67,689 AX. 8,444 A smoke 59,005 BX. 14,160 B Stair shell were dealt with at A.R.P. During July above A3560 AX 1108 BX&C 1440 was sent up by D.A.C. to positions of attached Artillery. + to position of 33 Bde A7482 AX 2436 BX&C 1968 Tous Bde A5090 AX 1632 BX&C 2244 Weight of ammunition handled even over 5,600 Tons	G.C.T.

M.S.L.H. Maud
Capt. & S.T.C.

CONFIDENTIAL.

8th DIVISIONAL ARTILLERY.

WAR DIARY

OF

8' Div'n Am Column

From 31.7 To 31.8.17

(VOLUME 34)

With Appendices Nos. ———

Vol 33

WAR DIARY
or
INTELLIGENCE SUMMARY

(Erase heading not required.)

Army Form C. 2118.

Volume IX

Place	Date	Hour	Summary of Events and Information	Remarks and references to Appendices
G.24.C.88	31-7-17		8 D.A.C.	
		14/15th July when S.A.A. dump was shelled. Rest on June 15 Limbered GS wagons with drawn team wagon line.	G.C.T.
	1-8-17		Orders received re handing over R dump @ Gordon House dump to 25th Div.	
			512 18 P @ 240 Bx delivered to 33 Bde. on pack arrival. 1 O.R. wounded @ 1 mile billet.	
	2.8.17		2/Lt W. Reynolds R.F.A. posted to 32nd Battery. 2/Lt. A.G. Lucas R.F.A. posted to 15th Battery	G.C.T.
			8 wagon loads of RE material sent up by 1 & 2 Section to forward Battery positions	
			512 18p @ 480 Bx packs from rear to forward batty positions. 1 O.R. Rifles 6 wounded 5 animals	
			killed 27 wounded. 480 18P packed up in same way G 33 R 9 1 R&1 mile wounded.	G.C.T.
	3.8.17		120 pack units of B echelon transferred to command of Capt Vivian. B half of pack animals of 1 & 2 section withdrawn to wagon lines. Rear wagon lines of D.A.C. withdrawn to old wagon line in Poperinghe area except Hd Nº 1 section took over old lines of 25 D.A.C. at G.21.Q.7.2.	G.C.T.
	4.8.17		Orders received for remainder of pack mules to rejoin their work being taken over by 58 D.A.C. All forward wagon lines returned by 1 p.m. Draft of 8 O.R. from Base, artillery Officer to 12'o exp 116 gn.	G.C.T.
	5-8-17		B.G.R.A. visited each section in turn, to congratulate them & thank them for the successful way in which the work of keeping up the Supply of Ammunition & material for road roads had been kept up in spite of the terrible conditions & hostile shell fire under which the work had been done.	G.C.T.
	6.8.17	11.30 p.m	Column inspected by G.O.C. 8th Division, who congratulated & thanked all ranks on work done	G.C.T.

WAR DIARY or INTELLIGENCE SUMMARY.

Army Form C. 2118.

Instructions regarding War Diaries and Intelligence Summaries are contained in F. S. Regs., Part II. and the Staff Manual respectively. Title pages will be prepared in manuscript.

(Erase heading not required.)

Place	Date	Hour	Summary of Events and Information	Remarks and references to Appendices
POPERINGHE	6/8/17	2.30 p.m.	S.D.A.C. Column inspected by Corps Commander Sir Claude Jacob K.C.B., who made a very congratulatory speech after inspecting the ranks.	G.C.T.
	7/8/17	10.30 a.m.	G.O.C. 8th Division presented ribbons to all who had been awarded them. 53650 Capt. WILLIS W awarded a parchment certificate for Gallantry & devotion to duty near YPRES	G.C.T.
			No. 104985 Dr. E. CALLOWAY awarded Military Medal for gallantry & devotion to duty	G.C.T.
8/8/17			Dvr A 27 sent to T.M. Batteries	G.C.T.
9/8/17			No. 94990 Sergt. C. LITTLE awarded Military Medal for gallantry & devotion to duty near ZILLEBEKE on 2nd August. 15 O.R. from Rear of column, 5 drivers remained with Column	G.C.T.
10/8/17			Party of 125 inc. from D.A.C., Brigades & Div. Train under Major L.B. MORTON R.F.A. sent to CALAIS to draw 250 mounts for 6 Div. Orders received re taking over K. dump H.23.a.3.2. ⊕ S. dump I.17.b.67 from 25th D.A. on 11th inst. Lieut. R.B. NUNN R.F.A. detailed to take charge. These 2 dumps being replaced by ARP by 2/Lt F. LEACH R.F.A.	G.C.T.
11/8/17			No. 31170 Sgt. C.A. GOODWIN & 17475 Corpl. MURRAY awarded Military Medal for gallantry & devotion to duty.	G.C.T.
			B Echelon reorganised as SAA section formed in packs & up generally.	
12/8/17			B Echelon sent up to L.G.S. wagons of S.A.A. to S. dump. Casualties 1 mule wounded	G.C.T.
13/8/17			2/Lt E.F. BRYAN R.F.A. returned to R.B. NUNN R.F.A. at K & S dumps. Whole of B Echelon less G.S. Wagons & SAA Carts only moved to forward wagon lines 13.O.R. 38 animals left behind. Pack animals of A Echelon	

WAR DIARY or INTELLIGENCE SUMMARY.

Army Form C. 2118.

Place	Date	Hour	Summary of Events and Information	Remarks and references to Appendices
POPERINGHE AREA	13/5/17		Col is now forward & stated with Italians under Capt. CE WOU MC RFA,	
	14/5/17		6 mules killed - wounded & 1 I.O.R. (12 minutes). Casualties 1 O.R. killed 3 O.R. wounded. Pack animals hard at work all day doing 3 trips each. Casualties 2/Lt E.F BRYAN RFA & 1.O.R wounded Gassed at duty. 5 O.R wounded to hospital. 40 O.R wounded at duty. 1.O.R missing.	G.C.T.
	15/5/17		Animals Killed 1 L.D & 6 mules - Wounded 1 Rider 12 mules Major L.B. Mouncer RFA relieved Capt C.E. Wing in charge of forward A Echelon. During the last 36 hours 44 L.G.S loads & 100 pack animals of S.A.A etc sent up also 130 & 1 S.P. & 740 B.X. on pack to Battery positions. Joined from Base. LT A.L MARR RFA 2/Lt. R.C.S. MEEK, J.M. FAIRBAIRNS, C.O. SMITH, R.L. NUNNEY, K.G. McMILLAN, W.E. WHITE RFA — 2/Lt. MEEK & 2/Lt FAIRBAIRNS RFA posted to D.A.C. other Sent direct to Brigade.	G.C.T.
	16/5/17		No 71940 Dr Riley found from 1st 2 Military prison on suspicion of desertion. Horse Dump H 24.6.13 taken over by LT NUNN RFA & RSM SIMMONS. 456 18P & 288 BX Delivered to 45th Bde in wagons. 3 O.R wounded 1 O.R Missing. 1 R & 6 mules Killed 8 mules wounded 400 Pack animals sent up to Batteries from forward wagon lines. 2/Lt E.F BRYAN RFA to hospital. Dapt A/RSM & 28 O.R joined from Base 10 O.R posted to 33 Bde 11 O.R to 45 Bde B.S.M to 1 Section vice A/BSM Thomas to 33 Bde.	G.C.T.

WAR DIARY
or
INTELLIGENCE SUMMARY.
(Erase heading not required.)

Army Form C. 2118.

Place	Date	Hour	Summary of Events and Information	Remarks and references to Appendices
POPERINGHE	16/8/17		428 Pack animals from forward w.L. to Battery positions. 1 mule killed. 2/Lt F.W.T. R.F.A. posted to 33 B⁹ Major G.R. Reid R.F.A. Rtts w.a. onc	G.C.T.
AREA	17/8/17		308 Pack animals from forward W.L. to Battery positions. 1 mule wounded. 6 O.R to hospital	G.C.T.
			Sick from B Echelon forward, probably shell shock.	G.C.T.
	18/8/17		150 pack animals sent up to forward positions. 2 mules wounded	G.C.T.
	19/8/17		160 pack animals sent up to gun line. No casualties	G.C.T.
	20/8/17		60 pack animals sent up to gun line. Two wagons on way up to 33B⁹ gun line caught by I shell close to Belgian chateau. 2/Lt J.M. FAIRBAIRNS R.F.A. @ O.R Killed. 3 O.R. wounded. 1 Rider ⊕ 4 mules killed, 1 Rider wounded, ⊕ missing. 3 mules wounded.	G.C.T.
	21/8/17		1 Wheels sent up with 3 gun wheels to put them on damaged guns in forward area. Salvage of Gun ⊕ wagons under taken by 6ᵗʰ D.A., Burial of animals by 25ᵗʰ D.A.	G.C.T.
	22/8/17		1 Wheels with 3 GS wheels sent up & on 21ˢᵗ	G.C.T.
	23/8/17		1 Wheels sent up with party from T.Ms to do repair work & salvage in forward area. 2/Lt. E.G.W. COWARD R.F.A	G.C.T.
	24/8/17	dec	2/Lt R.B. Munn R.F.A posted to 47 D.A.	G.C.T.
	25/8/17		All echelons refilled with Gun Amm⁰	G.C.T.
	27/8/17		2/Lt R.F. HUNT R.F.A 2/Lt W.F. Keating R.F.A joined from Base. 2/Lt E.G.W. Coward R.F.A posted to 45 Brigade	G.C.T.

WAR DIARY
or
INTELLIGENCE SUMMARY.

Army Form C. 2118.

(Erase heading not required.)

Place	Date	Hour	Summary of Events and Information	Remarks and references to Appendices
Poperinghe	28/7		& D.A.C. March orders received for D.A.C. to march to EECKE area on 29th inst.	G.C.T.
Area	29/7	7.15 a.m.	D.A.C. marched via Renninghelst & Godewaersvelde to billets. H.Q.R.A at GODEWAERVELDE. 40 Armour units arrived & were collected en route. D.A.C. arrived in billets about 10.30 a.m. H.Q. about 1½ mls E.A. STEENVOORDE on ABEELE Road. 47 D.A.C. took over Camps evacuated by & D.A.C.	G.C.T.
EECKE Area	31st		Advance party sent to reconnoitre new billets near BAILLEUL. 2/Lts CHAMBERS CAVERHILL and DARLING. R.F.A. joined from Base.	G.C.T.

[signature]

Army Form C. 2118.

8th Divl. Ammn. Column

VOLUME 34

WAR DIARY
or
INTELLIGENCE SUMMARY.
(Erase heading not required.)

Instructions regarding War Diaries and Intelligence Summaries are contained in F. S. Regs., Part II. and the Staff Manual respectively. Title pages will be prepared in manuscript.

Place	Date	Hour	Summary of Events and Information	Remarks and references to Appendices
EECKE AREA	Sept. 1	6 p.m.	8. D.A.C. DAC marched to BAILLEUL area arriving about 7.30 p.m. Sections in lines just south of main Hdqr Section lines	
			in tents. 211th CHARGERS RFA reported to DA	GCT.
BAILLEUL Area	2nd		Aeroplanes bombed area intermittently from 11 p.m. till 5 a.m. 2 Gunners in B Echelon lines killed. Sapanchs	
			Gassaulding 5. 1 man slightly wounded. 2/Lt. K. Wesley-Swift — A. Brodie — E.G. Clewlow — D. Glen —	GCT.
	3rd		Mt. Ituria RFA & 380R joined from Base. All officers posted direct to Brigade	
			280R posted to Brigade. Advance party sent on to reconnoitre lines to be taken over from New Zealand DAC in Steenwerck Area. 1 horse killed 1 man wounded by Aeroplane bomber 10 a.m.	GCT.
			IN BAILLEUL	
	6th	11.30 a.m.	DAC marched to Steenwerck Area. HQ at B.9.c. 4.2 just west ARMEPPE. 1 Section at B.9.c.b.7.	GCT.
			2 Section B.21.a.4.1 B Echelon at B.27.c.8.8. H.Q. Div. D R.A at Steenwerck.	
			A.R P at ROMARIN B.A.4.6. T. SAA Dump (80000) B.S.C.27 taken over by 21st CAVERHILL RFA with R.S.M	
			SIMMONS	
	8th		CAPT. OLIVER RFA went to BOULOGNE to draw remounts for 8th Division.	GCT.
	9th		A.836 AX.5.32 BX 288 sent up to 45 Bde position. Casualties NIL.	GCT.
	10th		A.1710 AX.1026 BX 282 sent up to gun position. 38 & 45 Bde. Casualties. NIL.	GCT.

Army Form C. 2118.

WAR DIARY
or
INTELLIGENCE SUMMARY.
(Erase heading not required.)

Instructions regarding War Diaries and Intelligence Summaries are contained in F.S. Regs., Part II. and the Staff Manual respectively. Title pages will be prepared in manuscript.

Place	Date	Hour	Summary of Events and Information	Remarks and references to Appendices
	Sept:		8th D.A.C.	
NEUFE	11		684 A 684 AX 288 BX sent up to Supplies Casualties Nil.	G.C.T.
	12		684A 684 AX 266 BX sent up to Gun positions Casualties NIL. 243 Ordnance Wagon TM Personnel	G.C.T.
	13		532 A 380 AX 276 BX Ami up to gun position. Casualties Nil. Capt. Olver returned sick reward	A.D.Q.
			for 8 Bn.	
	14		380 A 912 AX and 300 BX sent up to gun position - Casualties Nil. 30 Park Arty convoy Ammunition for 3rd Bn King's	A.D.Q.
	15		228 A/S Amd up to gun position. Casualties Nil.	A.D.Q.
	16		576 BX and 912 AX Amd up to gun position - Casualties Nil. to Park mules & T.M. Battery to remove ammunition	A.D.Q.
	17		228 A 228 AX and 288 BX Amd up to gun position - Casualties Nil	A.D.Q.
	18		144 BX and 144 B Smoke Amd up to gun position. Casualties Nil	A.D.Q.
	19		2/Lt J.M. Stoate relieved 2/Lt F.A.H. CAVERHILL at ARP ROMARIN DUMP and DOU-DOU BOMB DUMP. No ammunition sent up to gun position by D.A.C. Casualties NIL	T.O.D.
	20		An ammunition sent up to gun position by D.A.C. Casualties NIL	A.D.Q.
	21		An ammunition Amt up to gun position by DAC. Casualties 1 - 2= 238680 Gunner A Martland - wounded a/a - aircraft attack - Part of 46 OR 8 Bn. Arriving including draft renewal to R.S. Barn Renoin Depot CALAIS & 11 O.R. 8th D.A.C. under an A.S.C. officer proceeded to R.S. Barn Renoin Depot CALAIS & drawn renewals as follows - 8 - Bn. July 1 c. 73 L.D. - 14 Mules (including 16 S.L.D. 14 mules for 8 DAC)	A.D.Q.

WAR DIARY
or
INTELLIGENCE SUMMARY.
(Erase heading not required.)

Army Form C. 2118.

Place	Date	Hour	Summary of Events and Information	Remarks and references to Appendices
NIEPPE	21		Other Units 4 & 11 R. 13 L.D.	10 Q
	22		Gun ammunition was taken up to gun positions by D.A.C. Casualties NIL	10 Q
			Postings of Officers – R.A. 8th Bde R.O. 9: 260 dated 23/9/17 – 2/Lieut C.E.PROCTOR 3rd Battery R.F.A. posted to 8" Batt. with effect from 22.9.17 – posted to Bde 27 Section. 3/Lieut H.C.COUNSELL S" Battery R.F.A. posted to 8" D.A.C. with effect from 22-9-17 – posted to No. 1 Section.	10 Q
	23		Gun ammunition was taken up to gun positions by D.A.C. Casualties NIL	10 Q
	24		Gun ammunition was taken up to gun positions by D.A.C. Casualties NIL	10 Q
			2/Lieut E.A.H.CAVERHILL returned to "B" Echelon from DOU DOU DUMP. Remount for Division arrived from CALAIS – These allotted to R.F.A. were distributed to Sections by C.O. 8 D.A.C. as follows – horses L.D. 2 Mules 4 to 1 Section, Mules 8 to 2 Section, charger 1 horse G.C.T. L.D. 3 car ambce 2 to B. Echelon.	G.C.T.
	25		Gun ammunition was taken up to gun positions by D.A.C. Casualties NIL. 2/Lieut E.F. BRYAN returned from BASE.	
			13 Gunners & 2 Drivers posted to Brigades. No 2 Section start on new lines of B 25 c 2.5 Stables office in park huts to be built by R.E.	G.C.T.
	27		2/Lieut S.F. HILL R.F.A. posted to 45 Bde R.F.A.	G.C.T

Army Form C. 2118.

WAR DIARY
or
INTELLIGENCE SUMMARY.
(Erase heading not required.)

Place	Date	Hour	Summary of Events and Information	Remarks and references to Appendices
			3 DAC	
MIEPPE	Sept 24		2/Lt R.A. DARLING R.F.A. @ 2/Lt RE AGNT. RFA posted to X @ Y/c T.M. Batteries	G.C.T
			Except for the send of 1 to 18th when D/AC broke up A5932 AX 5358 DX 3186 to Ammunition	
			Column supplied 90 pack mules to collect Ammn. Column was twenty occupied in clearing	
			up camp which was left in readiness to duty @ in preparing Camp @ standing for	C.C.T
			winter.	

[signature]
(??) O/c D.A.C.

APPENDIX. A.

8th DIVISIONAL ARTILLERY.

CASUALTIES that have occurred in Personnel during Month ending 30th September 1917.

	33rd Brigade R.F.A.		45th Brigade R.F.A.		8th D.A.C.		Trench Mortars.	
	Officers.	O.R.	Officers.	O.R.	Officers.	O.R.	Officers.	O.R.
Strength on 1st					20	650		
SICK.					—	12		
KILLED.					—	1		
WOUNDED.					—	3		
INJURED.					—	—		
To Bdes etc					14	199		
Missing.								
ABSENTEES.					—	—		
TOTAL WASTAGE.					14	214		
Re-inforcements received.					12	265		
STRENGTH AT END OF MONTH.					18	701		

Comdg 8th Divl Ammn Coln. R.F.A.

WAR DIARY
or
INTELLIGENCE SUMMARY.
(Erase heading not required.)

Army Form C. 2118.

VOLUME 35

Place	Date	Hour	Summary of Events and Information	Remarks and references to Appendices
MERRE	Oct 2		2 C.O. Miles received from M.V.S. 10th office & N.C.O. detailed to attend cookery instruction in Armentiers 8th Oct 10th to 19th October. Instruction for 12 hours each day. 2/Lt H Walker RFA to train	G.C.T.
	4th		G.O.C. 8 Div. presented medal ribbon to Sergt Gordon, Corpl Murray (R. Section) also to all who had won in date. Blind cow had allowed personnel N° 2 Section moved to B 25 c 3.6	G.C.T.
			3GS Wagon Section to Salvo Empty Cases from Wagon. 3rd Battery position cut water to weather	G.C.T.
	5th		8 Div How slow started but was postponed a/c 1st Cavalry owing to weather	G.C.T.
	6th		Horse show continued. Mule Races B Echelon 1st - 2 sections tied - L Section 3rd. H Q 2nd in horse teams. 2 Scot.n 2nd in W.O. turn out & 1st in N.C.Os turn out & 3rd in men teams. B Echelon 2nd in Fire turn out 1 Section 1st 6 mule teams - 2 Section 3rd	G.C.T.
	8th		Programme of 6th caused out Col. F.W. Adeson RFA 1st in Officers Jumping. Guide is N.W.N - Capt. H.A Douglas RAMC second in our 1st hounds class. H.Q. D.A.C. 1st in Single horse turn out. 2/Lt P. Malson (Herring) 3rd in Jumping for N.C.Os (Herring). B.S.M. Flint (R Section) 1st in Championship R Sing hours. 2 Section 2nd in loading on trans back. B Echelon 1st Champion ship Mules	
			Total in D.A.C. 16 7 1st prizes - 7 2nd prizes & 4 3rd prizes	G.C.T.
			1 Mule wounded	
	14th		3GS wagon continued visiting to salve empty cases from lines 1st Battery position	G.C.T.

WAR DIARY
or
INTELLIGENCE SUMMARY.
(Erase heading not required.)

Army Form C. 2118.

Place	Date	Hour	Summary of Events and Information	Remarks and references to Appendices
	11th		Half of the animals in DAC went through Dip near Sloet weerde at rate of 58 per hour	GCT
	13th		2/Lt C.E. PROCTOR RFA posted to Lt 1/B	GCT
	15th		Men detailed for work at central Clipping Station sent to report for work at 86 RFA lines.	GCT
			Latrine station re-established	
	16th		2/Lt H.C. COONSELL RFA posted to Rt Bk & from J.K. HOWARD Harts Yeomanry joined as adviser in horse management	GCT
	17th		Orders received for 2/Lt F LEACH RFA to proceed home to take up work with Vickers Mills	GCT
	18th		2/Lt CAVEHILL RFA detailed for course in signalling at 2nd Army School ZUYTPEENE to start on 22nd inst.	CCT
	19th		5 O.R Detailed for a course of Signalling at TAHUKA Camp B.E.D 86 starting 24th	GCT
	20th		20 O.R detailed from B section Q B Echelon to work on building OP's for left group & to live with left group	GCT
	21st		10 O.R from B Section Q Section sent to Right Group to work on OP's & to live with the Brigade	GCT
	23rd		Capt S.C. TYLOR having been attached to HQRRA 8 Div Lt E.C. MILLER took up duties of adjutant 8th DAC temporarily	Eth.

Army Form C. 2118.

WAR DIARY
or
INTELLIGENCE SUMMARY.

(Erase heading not required.)

Vol. 35

Place	Date	Hour	Summary of Events and Information	Remarks and references to Appendices
NIEPPE	Oct 24		8th D.A.C.	
			1 L.D. made recess'd from M.V.S. Posted to No. 2 Sec.	Sch.
	25		No. 59605 Dr. A.W. RALPH wounded. One of the working party at O.P. for 2nd L.T. Group.	PCA.
	26		1 L.D. made recess'd from M.V.S. Posted to No. 3 Sec. Since 24th inst 1900 rounds 18½ ammunition fired	Sch.
	27		4.G.S. wagons handed over to 23rd Infantry Brigade for 1 week.	Sch.
	28		7 L.D. Horses. 4 Riders 5 Mules received from Base. Posted No. 1 L.D. No. 2 L.D. B Sch. as mules + ariders. HORSED PCR	
	29		2 L.D. from No. 3 were posted to 2nd Army units	Sch.
	30		2nd Lt. E.F. BRYAN detailed for 2nd Army Artillery School 11th Course	Sch.
	31		B² HOLLAND detached to a Course at 2nd Army F+B.T. School.	Sch.
			Since 28th June 30. O.R. have been working with the Brigade Laundry. O.R. Stores. The work Column has been principally occupied in improving and extending accommodation for men and animals. Repairing the camps in winter.	Sch.

M.R. Rutherford
Lt. Col. R.E.
(Comdg.)

APPENDIX.

8th DIVISIONAL ARTILLERY.

CASUALTIES that have occurred in Personnel during Month ending ...October 31, 1914...

	33rd Brigade R.F.A.		45th Brigade R.F.A.		8th D.A.C.		Trench Mortars.	
	Officers.	O.R.	Officers.	O.R.	Officers.	O.R.	Officers.	O.R.
Strength on 1st					18	401		
SICK.					1	4		
KILLED.								
WOUNDED.						1		
INJURED.						1		
To Bdes, etc.								
MISSING.					3	28		
ABSENTEES.						1		
TOTAL WASTAGE.					3	35		
Re-inforcements received.						24		
STRENGTH AT END OF MONTH.					15	690		

E.C. Miller
ADJUTANT, 8TH DIV^L AMM^N. COL^{MN}. R.F.A.

WAR DIARY or INTELLIGENCE SUMMARY
Army Form C. 2118.

8 D Amm Col
Vol 36

Place	Date	Hour	Summary of Events and Information	Remarks and references to Appendices
NIEPPE	Nov 1		8th D.A.C.	L.C.L.
	3		Lt R.S. LEWIS and 2/Lt R.C.S. MEEK detached to attend Gas course.	P.L.
	5		Capt. H.J. DARVILL attached to 8th A.A.C.	P.L.
	6		Twelve G.S. Wagons detached to cart bricks for R.E. work at waterpoints. 12 O.R. returned from VIII Corps L.C.R. Horse Sh. Sch.	P.L.
			Draft of 1 Sjt + 60 O.R. arrived from base	
	7		Draft of 15 O.R. arrived from base. 5 unposted to 45th Brigade. 10 to 33rd Brigade.	P.L.
	8		Lt W. ROWE to attend Gas course. vice Lt R.S. LEWIS.	
			1 Sergeant and 1 O.R. posted to 38th Brigade. 1 O.R. posted to 45th Brigade.	S.C.R.
			All detached men recalled to their units.	N.R.
	9		Capt. H.J. DARVILL returned to 33rd Div. Art'y.	P.L.
	10		8th D.A.C. marched via NEUVE EGLISE & KEMMEL to Wagon Line 2 miles East of POPERINGHE	P.L.
	11		8th Div. Artillery relieve Canadians in ZONNEBEKE Sect.	P.L.
			Capt. G. TYLER attached on Remount Staff Capt. at Rear H.Q. Div. Art'y.	
	12		Party under RSM sent forward to A.R.P. at WARWICK FARM (East of YPRES).	P.L.
	13		Received by March Pct 5 OR, 16 Riding Hy, 11 HD Draught.	P.C.L.
	14		Delivered by truck 33 Gunnels to 1st Bn May. 336 Gunnels to 32nd Bn May. 132 Gunnels to 45th May.	S.C.L.
	15		Capt. W.H. OLIVER posted to 1st Art. May. Capt. I.T.H. DAVISON took over B Echelons 8th D.A.C.	P.C.L.

WAR DIARY or INTELLIGENCE SUMMARY

Army Form C. 2118.

Vol. 36

33rd D.A.C.

Place	Date	Hour	Summary of Events and Information	Remarks and references to Appendices
Popringhe	Mar 15		LT E.C. MILLER took over duties of Adjutant 8th A.C. Amplewarp. LT E.A. STOCKEN posted to 33rd Brigade.	
			Delivered by pack 664 rounds to 33rd Batty. 336 rounds to 3rd Batty. 261 rounds to 57 Batty.	P.Ch.
	16		Draft of 15 Drivers arrived from Base. Shell fell in Bickern lines abandoned Gun killed 87587 Dr AMBLER.F. and mule "Bell". 12124 Dr S.Penny (shell shock) and also L.D. Animals. also wounded 111324 Dr VARLEY.T.T. and wounded 5 Gunners. On driver to 33rd Bgd. 4 to driver to HQ Bde. Delivered by pack 336 rounds to 3rd 132 rounds 633rd Bde.	F.Ch. / F.Ch.
	17		Delivered by pack 600 rounds to 3rd Battery	S.C.M.
	18		Delivered by pack 672 rounds to 3rd Battery. 86239 Dr LAWRENCE.E. wounded.	P.Ch.
	19		Delivered by pack 672 rounds to 3rd Battery. 1 mule killed. 3 Scts arrived from Base. posted to Brigade	P.Ch.
	20		Delivered by pack 672 rounds to 3rd Battery. Casualties 62065 Dr SNEDDON wounded. 43884 Dr DAVEY wounded.	P.Ch.
			62395 Dr DILLON.G. wounded. 50526 Dr SUMMERS H. killed in action. 9 mules killed. 8 mules reported.	P.Ch.
	22		Woodenwich abandoned. Lost horses. 35 horses out on various fatigues.	P.Ch.
	24		672 rounds delivered by pack to 33rd Battery. Draft of 12 Drivers & 3 Gunners arrived from Base	P.Ch.
	25		664 rounds delivered by pack 6 & 8 Bde Hdqrs. LT J.M. SLADE to England Medical Board	S.Ch.
	26		664 rounds delivered by pack 33rd Battery. 67 Drivers posted to Brigades. 4th 2 Drivers 8 1st D'Amr + 2 Ribs.	P.Ch.
	27		672 rounds delivered by pack. 39 Sc Bde. H.Q. 39 various duties. Round Wood detachment for a Siv.	P.Ch.
			Base — Ammunition Column No 642 reinforced. On 7 packed by A.O in officer. Column now consists of MWS	
			of 142 Bullion carrying 16/CLAC Ammunition and S.A.A. section carrying only S.A.A. + grenades, milk only 4 given at the Beach Wagon — carry extra technical stores in P.S. wagon and also outer body wagon	WMS

Army Form C. 2118.

WAR DIARY
or
INTELLIGENCE SUMMARY.
(Erase heading not required.)

Vol 36

Place	Date	Hour	Summary of Events and Information	Remarks and references to Appendices
			8" D.A.C	
Popenysth	Nov 27		Draft of 118 Gunners received from Base.	P.t.h.
	27		2nd LT J. McINTYRE and 2nd LT T. McLEOD joined from Base. 2nd Lt J. McINTYRE posted to 37th Battery	P.t.h.
	28		MAJOR L.B. MONTRESOR evacuated to Hospital. Capt. T.H. DAVISON took over No. 2.S.C Reinforcl. + Lt W. ROWE 108K over S.A.A. See reinforcements. Delivered 336 rounds to 1st Battery. 336 rounds to 5" Battery. 15 - 2 rounds to 37" Battery & ped.	P.t.h
	29		Delivered by pack 336 rounds to 1st Battery. 336 rounds to 5" Battery. 152 Rounds to 37" Battery.	S.t.h.
	30		One horse wounded by shellfire on the limber during night 29/30 ft. Delivered by pack 336 rounds to 1st Battery. 336 rounds to 5.4" Battery. Held convoy of pny 20 whones of D.R. HARVEY. S.t.h. 11607 Dr. W.E. KEWISH. Killed. 2 mules killed + 2 wounded whilst taking up ammunition. R.h. Lt Col. LORD WYNFORD attached to this unit. Since 12th Nov. this unit took up 19,876 rounds to Battery Positions. also carried a large quantity of R.E. material for Battery positions. also attend up the camps. Casualties o.R. 3 killed. 6 wounded. Mules 12 killed. 13 wounded.	P.t.h.

AMWhiteland
Cap? 8" DAC

APPENDIX.

8th DIVISIONAL ARTILLERY.

CASUALTIES that have occurred in Personnel during Month ending November 30th 1917

	33rd Brigade R.F.A.		45th Brigade R.F.A.		8th D.A.C.		Trench Mortars.	
	Officers.	O.R.	Officers.	O.R.	Officers.	O.R.	Officers.	O.R.
Strength on 1st					15	690		
SICK.					1	120		
KILLED.						3		
WOUNDED.						5		
INJURED. To Brigade					6	145		
MISSING.								
ABSENTEES.						1		
TOTAL WASTAGE.					7	174		
Re-inforcements received.					4	80		
STRENGTH AT END OF MONTH.					12	596		

Schuller B.
ADJUTANT, 8TH DIVL. AMMN. COLMN.
for O.C.

Army Form C. 2118.

WAR DIARY
or
INTELLIGENCE SUMMARY.
(Erase heading not required.)

Vol 37

Place	Date	Hour	Summary of Events and Information	Remarks and references to Appendices
Potchefstroom	Dec. 1		S.A.F.A.	
			Delivered by pack 336 rounds to 1st Battery	P.L.
	2		Delivered by pack 336 rounds to 5th Battery. MAJOR. L.R. MONTREFOR. R.F.A. Chuck off Ship Ill. in England.	S.L.
	3		Delivered by pack 336 rounds to 32nd Battery, 336 rounds to 33rd Battery, 132 rounds to 1st Battery, 4.5" Battery	S.L.
			2/Lt ENWOOD joined from England. Posted to 33rd Battery A/4 B	P.L.
	4		Delivered by pack 336 rounds to 32nd Battery, 336 rounds to 33rd Battery, 336 rounds to 53rd Battery, 128 rounds to 5" Battery	
			#7119. Dr. BOULET and 1394 B. HULL. J. wounded. 3 mules L.D. wounded.	P.L.
	5		Draft of 45 Drivers Ammunition Base	P.L.
			Reorganization of Horses. Mules &c. Pack Pack Ponies are required for remounts. 31 Drivers posted to Brigade	P.L.
	6		Delivered by pack 656 rounds to 36th Battery, 336 rounds to 1st Battery, 12 wdown to 4.5" Battery, Col: BOTELER left for	
			a month's leave to England. Capt. C.E. VIVIAN. M.C. R.F.A. took over Command of 8th A.C. temporarily.	P.L.
	7		Lt. Col LORD WYNFORD left for F. 32nd Division. Delivered by pack 336 rounds 4.5" Battery, 336 rds. to 13th Battery. 124 Rounds to 57th Battery	P.L.
	8		Delivered by pack to 33rd Battery 336 rounds, to 1st Battery, 336 rounds to 53rd Battery. 124 rounds, 1 Mule killed, 1 Mule Battery, Sick from	P.L.
	10		2 B.S. sergeants detailed for Salvage of Ammunition duty	P.L.
	11		2 Drafts proceed from Base 1 of 6 gunners 4 of 3 of hostel to Brigade 2nd of 3 gunners 18/12, 51 posted to Brigade 2 posted to D.A.C.	P.L.
	11		2nd Lt. H. HUTCHINGS and 2/Lt. T.C. DOGERTY joined from Base. 2/Lt. J.H. HIBBERT joined for service with 1st A.S. Battery	P.L.
	12		2nd Lt. EGGLETON joined from Base. Posted to 36th Battery	P.L.

Army Form C. 2118.

WAR DIARY
or
INTELLIGENCE SUMMARY.
(Erase heading not required.)

Instructions regarding War Diaries and Intelligence Summaries are contained in F. S. Regs., Part II. and the Staff Manual respectively. Title pages will be prepared in manuscript.

8ᵗ D A C.   Vol. 37

Place	Date	Hour	Summary of Events and Information	Remarks and references to Appendices
POPERINGHE	Dec 13		Delivered by pack 152 rounds to 53ᵈ Battery & 152 rounds to 57ᵗ Battery	8ᵗ L
	14		Delivered by pack 152 rounds to 53ᵗ Battery. By wagons to first railway material to forward area	F.L.
	15		wagons by railway material to forward area	O.L.
	16		do. 1 Bt & 9 O.R. trailer joined from Base & posted 53ᵈ Bde 1 O.R. 64ᵗ	
	17		126ᵗ A. B. A.C. attached to DAC. Sent up railway material to forward area. 6 Gas joined from CW	
			Base & posted to 45ᵗ Bde R.F.A	
	18		32 Gen joined from Base 6 & posted to 53ᵗ Bde 3 do to 30ᵗ Bde Orders to	
			move to WINNEZEELE AREA received D.A.C filled up to complete	L.L
			establishment. Lt A CROPPER RFA joined from Base	
	19		N°1 Sec marched to WINNEZEELE AREA. 30 do posted to 119ᵗ Army Bde	R.L
			RFA	
	20		86ᵗ Army Bde R.F.A relieved 32ᵗ Bde (less 1 Battery)	RL
	21		HQ 8.2. Cdn posted DAC marched to WINNEZEELE AREA. HQ billet	R.L.
			at OUDEZEELE. N°1 Sec J.14. C.1.4 N°2 Sec C 3. d 3.7 SAA Sec C 30 a 2.8	
OUDEZEELE	25		2ᵈ Lieut T.A MOSS RFA joined from Base	H.O
	26		Complete Overhauling of Vehicles, Musketry Training and Pack Mule Training commenced month during period of rest	H.O

A6913 Wt. W11422/M1160 350,000 12/16 D. D. & L. Forms/C./2118/14.

WAR DIARY
or
INTELLIGENCE SUMMARY.

(Erase heading not required.)

Army Form C. 2118.

Vol 37

Place	Date	Hour	Summary of Events and Information	Remarks and references to Appendices
OUDEZEELE	28		Lieut: E.F. BRYAN R.F.A. posted to 33rd Bn. R.G.A. commanding 141° Bn RGA	JGB
			" E.A.H. CAVERHILL R.G.A. posted to 45th Bn R.G.A.	JGB
	29		" G. GILBERT RGA joined from base	JGB
			Orders received for 2nd DA to proceed to relieve 14 DA	JGB

G.W. Nixon
a/o Capt R.G.A.
C.R.G. 2nd Div. Ammn Col.

WAR DIARY
or
INTELLIGENCE SUMMARY.

Army Form C. 2118.

VOL 38.

Place	Date	Hour	Summary of Events and Information	Remarks and references to Appendices
VLAMERTINGHE	1918 Jany 1		Advance party to relief of 8 to 14 D.A.C. leaves.	
	2		8th D.A.C. marched from OUDERZEELE via WATOU + POPERINGHE to 14 D.A.C. lines.	
			Son A/U VLAMERTINGHE. Relief completed.	
			2nd Lt T.A. DRISCOLL joined from Base.	Sch.
	5		2nd Lt T.A. CROPPER took over Gun & ammunition Dumps, PICKERING, OXFORD.	Sch.
	7		8th B.A.C. took over XIII Corps Gun Pool from 30th D.A. 2nd Lt A. MOSS in Charge.	Sch.
			8th D.A.C. took over ORILLIA Dump. 2nd Lt Hy STACK H. HUTCHINSON in charge.	Sch.
	8		2nd Lt J.J. McLEOD and NCO & Orderly. Rest. See Courses (circular 13 men.)	Sch.
			2nd Lt GILBERT + party of 20 men attached to 254 Tunnelling Coy	Sch.
	9		123,889 Gnr SWANNELL A. wounded by Shell fire. Draft of 2 Drivers arrived from Base.	Sch.
	11		Col. F.W. BOTELER returned from leave & resumed Command.	Sch.
	12		Course for the care of Tyres started, in all 12 men detailed to attend.	Sch.
	14		Draft of 13 men arrived from Base, 12 Sent on to Brigades	
	16		Draft of 11 gnrs 33 men arrived from Base. 4 sent to Brigades.	
			2nd Lt L. JELLINEK arrived from leave.	Sch.
	17		Parties detailed for salving ammunition at Old Battery positions	Sch.
	21		D.A.C. relieved by 29th D.A.C. D.A.C. marched to POPERINGHE Reserve area	Sch.

WAR DIARY or INTELLIGENCE SUMMARY

Army Form C. 2118.

Place	Date	Hour	Summary of Events and Information	Remarks and references to Appendices
POPERINGHE	24		Draft of 9 Signallers from Base posted to 33rd Bde. R.F.A.	
			Major C.M. Asbury R.F.A. & 2/Lt. A.D. Roberts R.F.A. arrived from Base posted to 33rd Bde.	G.C.T.
			45th Bde. approved. Fatigue of 1 Offr. & 40 O.R. found daily to work on WELTJE.	
	25		C.O.C. R.A. 45th Bde. Arty. inspected wagon lines.	G.C.T.
	26		Orders received to move to new wagon lines.	G.C.T.
	27			G.C.T.
	28		Move to new wagon lines postponed. No movement carried out except for movement of B.D.A.C. moved to new camp 8.30 a.m. H.Q. at A.22.D.7.5. No. 1 Section at G.36.4.9. No. 2 Section at A.28.D.27. S.A.A. Section at A.28.C.3.6. (Sheet 28)	G.C.T.
	29		Draft of 18 Gunners 18 pr. 8 Gunners 4.5 1 Signaller from Base.	G.C.T.
	30		20 Gunners 18 pr. 15 Signallers & 8 Gunners 4.5 sent to Brigade.	G.C.T.

APPENDIX. A.

8th DIVISIONAL ARTILLERY.

CASUALTIES that have occurred in Personnel during Month ending January 31st 1918.

	33rd Brigade R.F.A.		45th Brigade R.F.A.		8th D.A.C.		Trench Mortars	
	Officers.	O.R.	Officers.	O.R.	Officers.	O.R.	Officers.	O.R.
Strength on 1st					14	582		
SICK.					-	11		
KILLED.					-	-		
WOUNDED.					-	1		
INJURED.					-	-		
To Bdes: etc:					3	78		
MISSING.					-	-		
ABSENTEES.					-	1		
TOTAL WASTAGE.					3	91		
Re-inforcements received.					7	111		
STRENGTH AT END OF MONTH.					18	602		

30-1-1918.

Wh?ul?ypl Major R.F.A.
For O.C. 8th D.A.C.

Army Form C. 2118.

WAR DIARY
or
INTELLIGENCE SUMMARY.
(Erase heading not required.)

8th Div Amm Col

VOLUME 30. Vol 39

8th D.A.C.

Place	Date	Hour	Summary of Events and Information	Remarks and references to Appendices
POPERINGHE	February 1-2-18		Daily fatigue of 4 wagons working for 158 Bde I forward area still continues	G.C.T.
	6.2.18		Dept of 28 O.R. from Base	G.C.T.
	8.2.18		Inspection of Column distinguished by C.R.A. Cold Shoer Bayts standing over three it was	G.C.T.
			Cancelled. Very good turn out. Orders received to relieve of 29th D.A. by it on 12-2-18	G.C.T.
	9.2.18		Morning Parade by G.O.C. 8th D.A. by G.O.C. 8th Div. between 9.30 & 12.30 Calculate about	G.C.T.
			round roads. Cancelled as G.O.C. was unable to attend.	G.C.T.
	10-2-18		A/Lt C.E.W.Jones R.F.A. joined from Base.	G.C.T.
	11-2-18		2/Lt RC & MEEK R.F.A. posted to 3rd Battery 2/Lt HASTOWE R.F.A. posted to S.A.A. Section	G.C.T.
	12.2.18		Capt. R.S.LEWIS R.F.A. 2nd/Lt T.A.MOSS R.F.A. No 11257 Sergt WESTLAKE R.E. No 47346 Corpl.	
			WEBSTER T.S. No 4817 Bdr MAHON M and No 30656 Trumpeter KILROY T detailed	
			to proceed to ROUEN Indian Cavalry Base Depot for course of training in	
			handling Indians. On 15th inst. 1 Officer & 2 N.C.Os to proceed to MARSEILLES	
			after course to bring back party of Indians according to establish up a D.A.C.	
			consisting partly of British partly Indian personnel	G.C.T.
	13-2-18		Draft of 11 Drivers and 2 signallers from Base 2/Lt S.L. BOORMAN RFA(T.F.) joins from Base	G.C.T.
	14.2.18		8 D.A.C. marched to ROAD CAMP VLAMERTINGHE moving from supper with line	G.C.T.

WAR DIARY
or
INTELLIGENCE SUMMARY.
(Erase heading not required.)

Army Form C. 2118.

Instructions regarding War Diaries and Intelligence Summaries are contained in F. S. Regs., Part II. and the Staff Manual respectively. Title pages will be prepared in manuscript.

Place	Date	Hour	Summary of Events and Information	Remarks and references to Appendices
	15/1/15		Taking over from 29th D.A.C. 2/Lt DOUGHTY RFA in charge of Oxford Dumps.	G.C.T.
			2/Lt DRISCOLL RFA posted to 45 B.J.	
			4 lorries to report daily to D.A.C. to assist in carrying tricks for station	G.C.T.
			Exchange of 15 O.R. arranged with 45 B.J. to replace men who are old or weak &c	
			200v how Gun Limb.	
	16/1/15		6 G.S. Wagons detailed daily to camp R.E. Material for Infantry	G.C.T
	18/1/15		2 Squadrons + Driver 6 New Gunners & Corpl 1 Bombardier 10/1/B.5? arrives	
			from Base Pierce posted to 13. J. Driver to O.K.	G.C.T
	20/1/15		2/Lt BERESFORD 2/Lt GODEN RFA arrived from Base posted to D.A.	G.C.T.
			Orders received for Capt. G.C. TYLOR RFA to be posted to 51" D.A. as S.C. RA out	
			2/Lt G. GILBERT RFA took over duties temporarily.	G.C.T
	21/1/15		Capt. G.C. TYLER left 8th 846 the pm. 57th Div Bty. 2/Lt. Rams struck off strength	B9
	23/1/15		2nd Beresford posted from 8 S.B.6 to 32 Batty 3 S.Siege RGA	B9
	24/1/15		Grooms and their horses for Capt. G.C. TYLER left 8th 846 to report to 51"XB	
			Daily Patterns of Surgeons carrying R.E. Material for Infantry, continue to B.	
	25/1/15		2/Lt Thomas and 2 Lt. Tachround reported from base	

Army Form C. 2118.

WAR DIARY
or
INTELLIGENCE SUMMARY.
(Erase heading not required.)

Instructions regarding War Diaries and Intelligence Summaries are contained in F. S. Regs., Part II. and the Staff Manual respectively. Title pages will be prepared in manuscript.

Place	Date	Hour	Summary of Events and Information	Remarks and references to Appendices
	25/9/18		2Lt THOMAS and 2Lt MacCORMACK posted to 1st and 33 Batteries	(B)
	26/2/18		Capt OLIVER joined R.H.Q. from 61 Batty. 2Lt WAYRE drawing Penis Hilts to Batteries 2Lt GORDON relieved 2Lt BOORMAN at Blythe (Townelly Camp)	(B)
	28/9/18		6 GS Wagons detailed to remove Indian Mule Cart & to 33 Batteries. Same supplied by Batteries. 1 GS Wagon sent to 35 Battery to replace one unyonwater repair.	(B)

(Sgd) M. Sutherland
Maj S. B. RFA

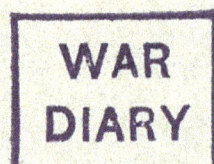

8th DIVISIONAL AMMUNITION COLUMN, R.A.

M A R C H

1 9 1 8

WAR DIARY
or
INTELLIGENCE SUMMARY.
(Erase heading not required.)

Army Form C. 2118.

8 DAC Vol 40

Place	Date	Hour	Summary of Events and Information	Remarks and references to Appendices
VLAMERTINGHE	1/3/18		8 DAC Came in Lorry Bus for 2 Gunners of the Section at 8AIB HQ., 22 T	
			WATERHOUSE of which Baker be AA station	
	2/3/18		2 Wagons despatch the Divisar Train Head Qtr Batteries	
	4/3/18		LT DAVIES. Who one on leave expired & 2/Lt. 261 GILBERT reported to SAA station LT BANNATYNE attached to Hairincourt	
	5.3.19		0	
	6.3.19		CRA inspected lines in morning. G.O.C. inspected lines in afternoon. Orders received from DA	
			re working Park P. 8 M r (BM 28/7(1) — 12 Wagons Rs distributed to Nissen huts for BCs	
	7.3.18		Orders received from Advance park to meet Staff Officer tomorrow at 9h.15	
	8.3.18		Working park 1 S Officers and 260 OR reported at SUNDERLAND Camp. 12 d arrived at 10 AM D.A.C. Proceed 1 Officer 70 OR 42 horses to GS wagons 2/Lt GILBERT officer detailed to look after officers & men in camp. DAC (A252s etc) responsible for rations to athletic camp	
			8th DV AAth have to look after 8th DAC march out at 9.30 AM and proceed to car to	
POPERINGHE EVERDINGHE	9.3.19		A28 and A22d. G38 vacated by divisin unit (39th DAC) - Summer time adopted last Km advanced one hour at 11 P.M. - Swifter huts detter R. bus & first necessitate states to 5 battery an advanced patch have to add at on have notice. The chief Inset. hatwa	

WAR DIARY
or
INTELLIGENCE SUMMARY.
(Erase heading not required.)

Army Form C. 2118.

Place	Date	Hour	Summary of Events and Information	Remarks and references to Appendices
	10/3		Sunday. Parade C.E. service 12 noon. O. a O.R. or URDU coming at Rouen return	[sgd]
	11.3.18		General cleaning up — Rumour of Batterys move to back area & away from present sector.	[sgd]
	12.3.18		Six Waynes G.S. sent collecting Nissen huts for 33rd Bde.	[sgd]
	15.3.18		Draft of 21 O.R. from Base	[sgd]
	14.3.18		Lft W.H.Pye to No. 2 section from 29th D.A.C. — 2/Lt Hull from 3rd Bde, to No 1 section	[sgd]
			2/Lt Whitehouse from SAA to 3rd Bde.	[sgd]
	15.3.18		Gunners from east R'ly as required GODEWAERSVELDE R'ly station for hostile entraining purposes	[sgd]
	16.3.18		Draft of 28 O.R. from Base	[sgd]
	17.3.18		Lt E. Ross gone for hospital in attached to No. 1 section	[sgd]
	18.3.18		C.O. inspected all sections	[sgd]
	19.3.18		Brig-Gen. LAMONT CMG DSO appointed as C.R.A.	[sgd]
	20.3.18		C.R.A. visit to Ammn. Col.	[sgd]
	21.3.18		Much enemy active known — the situation has a momentous interest	[sgd]
	22.3.18		Mon. of 8th Dn Artillery, No 2 Section entrain with 33rd Bde R.F.A. at GODEWAERSVELDE Siding Ang 1 Section entrain with 45th Bde from HOUPLINES siding — DAC HQ with HQ RA and Dn. Kam from HOUPLINES — SAA Section entrain in 2 parts for HOUPLINES and GODEWAERSVELDE	[sgd]
			C.O. injured by fall for horse on 21st for & Rest camp – Capt Vivian MC assumes command	

Army Form C. 2118.

WAR DIARY
or
INTELLIGENCE SUMMARY.
(Erase heading not required.)

Place	Date	Hour	Summary of Events and Information	Remarks and references to Appendices
GUILLAUCOURT	23.3.18		Section action during day at VILLERS BRETONNEUX – MARCELCAVE – GUILLAUCOURT. HQ with the lead 2 Sections west of GUILLAUCOURT. Considerable difficulty was felt in concentrating Brigades	Apps
	24.3.18		SAA section arrive 3 AM & handed up horses & mules 2/3 of train surrendered to Infy Btns to the line. About 9.30 PM a scout travelling from Abancourt and stragglers that German cavalry were advancing in the village in considerable strength. Scouts observing and generally destroying the peace for our trains. – O.C. SAA section 2/Lt STONE.	Apps
CAIX	25.3.18		DAC moves to CAIX. No 1 & 2 Sections coming 24 and 12 Wagon load of Ammn respectively to 33rd and 45th Bdes. O.C. No 1 Section Lt. ROSS O.C. No 2 Section Capt OLIVER	Apps
MARCELCAVE IGNAUCOURT	26.3.18		DAC moved to MARCELCAVE & remain 2 hrs & then proceeded to IGNAUCOURT. No 1 & 2 section having "Aichilon" escarpe on CAYEUX – CAIX Rd near B15 Wagon lines.	Apps
IGNAUCOURT	27.3.18		HQ and all G Sections from No 1 & 2 section move at 10.30 PM to AUBERCOURT where "B" Echelon started and is filled up from MT lorries. 23rd Bde AFA Am Col and 16"KHA BAC come under 8th D.A.C.	Apps
AUBERCOURT	28.3.18	8 AM	Move to Xrd AMIENS – ROYE – AMIENS – MORCUIL – DEMUIN (HQ, B Echelon & SAA section). No 1 & 2 section are when about 3 & 4.5th Bdes move with them & have Lt HILL and 1/Lt BOORMAN as liaison officers for ammunition supply. Hereafter. At 1 PM DAC move to Rd Junction E of MOREUIL but immediately sent to take a firm over Rouvrel & Moisenceailly Rd. Hostilities settle this after a further move to ORESMAUX is ordered. The great	Apps

WAR DIARY
or
INTELLIGENCE SUMMARY.
(Erase heading not required.)

Army Form C. 2118.

Place	Date	Hour	Summary of Events and Information	Remarks and references to Appendices
JUMEL			retreat of enemy cancelled wait along the main road. Wonderfully carried out at night. No troops going to Reserve pts forward where short to take over a part of the line. DAC on way to ORESMAUX were checked at JUMEL and remain. We went running. DAC with Bedelm its own Echelon	
AILLY	29.3.18		again returning to AILLY & then to ROUVREL (Mon DEE). SAA Section remain at JUMEL and on left with orders of Bn to "Q" applied spot from DA. Only a couple of hours at Mon IDEE	
ROUVREL			and flying in enemy. HQ & "B" echelon to "A" HALTE near THEZY-HAILLES - Aechelon (No M = 2	
THEZY			Section) moving from forward locations get involved in general officer confusion & do not reach the destination allotted to them. Their whereabouts unknown for 24 hrs.	
ST NICHOLAS	30.3.18	6 AM	HQ & Bedelm marched to ST NICHOLAS near BOYES - Capt VIVIAN reces with fatigue in advance for BOYES on arrival. 2/Lt PYE in command Bedelm Answer given through stretch near Bedelm for which Aechelon refered badly to up with about some after litres of ammunition by lettins. Units under 8th DAC and in whole 16th KHA BAC - 23rd AFABAC and 251 AFABAC	
	31.3.18		Location: HQ DAC near XXth BOYES-BLANGY-AMIENS-DOMART	
			Bedelm do. do.	
			Aechelon (No 1 Section) HAILLES	
			Aechelon (No 2) 23rd AFA BAC - HAILLES	
			FOUENCAMPS	
			Refer to Map AMIENS 17 100,000	

B.R.Davies Capt
an1 8 DAC.

14 8th Divisional Artillery.   Appendix K.

Casualties that have occurred in Personnel during Month ending 31/3/18.

	33rd Brigade R.F.A.		45th Brigade R.F.A.		8th D.A.C.		8th T.M.B.	
	O.	O.R.	O.	O.R.	O.	O.R.	O.	O.R.
Strength on 1st.					17	583.		
Sick					—	8.		
Killed.					—	1		
Wounded.					—	3		
Injured.					—	1		
To Base Sh.					1	42		
Absentees.					—	1		
Total Wastage					1	54		
Reinforcements					3	49		
Strength at End of Month.					19	578		

6/4/18.

A.A. Hung
2/Lt: R.F.A.
Adjt: for O.C. 8th D.A.C.
2/Lt: R.F.A.

8th Divisional Ammunition Column. Appendix.......

Casualties that have occurred in Personnel during Month ending 31st March 1918.

Strength on 1st		Reinforcements		Sick.	Killed	Wounded	Missing	Missing Absent	Total Wastage.	Strength at End of Month.	
Officers	O.R's. O.O.R.	Rec. O.O.R.	Posted to units etc. O.O.R.						O.O.R.		O.O.R.
14	583	3. 49.	1. 42.	8	—	3	1	—	1.54.	19.	578.

Signed.

2/Lieut: R.F.A.
Adjutant for O.C. 8th D.A.C.

Date. 6/4/18.

8th Divisional Artillery.

8th DIVISIONAL AMMUNITION COLUMN R.F.A.

APRIL 1918.

WAR DIARY or INTELLIGENCE SUMMARY

8th Div. Amm^n Column   Vol. 4.

Place	Date	Hour	Summary of Events and Information	Remarks and references to Appendices
	APRIL			
St Nicholas	1		With the situation now settled to a great degree, TH MO (Capt. DOUGLAS RAMC) returned to A/Amn unit	
	2		Two forward Dump stations FOUENCAMPS with 1st BIBBY TMB/y in charge and GENTELLES with 2/Lt CROPPER in charge. SAA section open with the Division into back area	
	3		Quiet day. Generally ammunition of all kinds still heavy so temporary storage at small camps and centralization	
	4		Forward Dumps moved back to St Nicholas and Crossroads. BOVES – BLANGY – AMIENS – DOMART R^ds	
BOVES	5		HQ "B" Ech^n suddenly ordered to move in convoy to N end of BOVES on BOVES-CAGNY R^d. No accommodation but found in room in 50 Div ASC Train. 2/Lt CROPPER relieved by 2/Lt MOSS at H.Q. of Dump at Gentelles	
	6		Various officers 9 O.R. return to Div Artillery from leave etc after having been detained at Base	
	7		G.S. wagons from "B" Ech^n collect extra pairs of horses from old Gun positions	
	8		C.O. returns from hospital. Nos 1 & 2 Sections (Q.F.) move back to Waggon lines near Bedelon	
	9		12 G.S. wagons back from Amm^n to 1st & 3 BAC	
	10		Take on following of A.C.C. Training 50 Div ASC Butler to 18 Div Bath for all men	
	11		24 QF loads 18 pdr to 45th Bde Tu 2/Lt JELLINEK return	
	12		12 QF loads 18 pdr to 45th Bde. Sent 18 m^ds to 33rd & 56 & 45 & 15 Bde R.F.A. Officers at Dumps:-	
			R&front:- 2/Lt DARLING TMB, 2/Lt JELLINEK. In front:- 2/Lt MOSS, 2/Lt LATIMER TMB.	

WAR DIARY
or
INTELLIGENCE SUMMARY.

(Erase heading not required.)

Army Form C. 2118.

Instructions regarding War Diaries and Intelligence Summaries are contained in F. S. Regs., Part II. and the Staff Manual respectively. Title pages will be prepared in manuscript.

Place	Date	Hour	Summary of Events and Information	Remarks and references to Appendices
	APRIL			
BOVES	12		9 QF Loads 16th [Bde] to 5th Bde — 2/Lt Hill relieves 2/Lt JELLINEK at Rt. Group Dump, ST NICHOLAS	
	13		12 QF Loads Ammn collected from 3rd Ygds advanced position & brought to reserve position	
	14		No 2 Section clean 3rd Ygds advanced position	
	15		2/Lt DUNNETT T.M.B. relieves 2/Lt DARLING at Rt Group dump	
	16		16th Div Arty march to VERS & spend night there. 4th Army Refill ammn	
	17		8th Div Arty march to LIERCOURT area, via CLAIRY - BOVANES - PICQUIGNY - HANGEST -	
GRANDSART			D.A.C. go to GRANDSART — 25 reservists collected at PICQUIGNY	
	18		Firing returns submitted	
	19.20		Refitting. Overhauling of waggons etc	
	21		2 18 pdrs & 1 4.5 How sent from each Bde to No 1 & 2 sections for drill purposes	
	22		5 Gunner Reinforcements and 21 Remounts	
	23		No 1 Sec. 5 men to make lines at EROMDELLE 10 NCOs posted 9 Sect to Batteries	
	24		Draft of 22 [men] for No 1 — 13 drivers for No 2. 11 K.I. posted to Batteries.	
	25		Inspection of No 1 & 2 sections & HQ in full marching order by G.M.A. & C.R.A. who then inspected Rt. Bde & 109 Gp Park, a preview of No. 2 section and in afternoon held firefights at drillads, spotting Rifles, Ammunition	
	26		Draft of 3 drivers for 45th Bde. Draft of 3 fitters, 1 wheeler, 12 S.S. a.r.t to Bdes (1 S.S. retained by Hd Section)	

A6945 Wt. W14422/M1160 350,000 12/16 D. D. & L. Forms/C./2118/14.

Army Form C. 2118.

WAR DIARY
or
INTELLIGENCE SUMMARY.
(Erase heading not required.)

Place	Date	Hour	Summary of Events and Information	Remarks and references to Appendices
GRANDSART	MARCH 27		HQrs + No 2 Section moved to ERONDELLE leaving at 10AM arriving 11.15AM. CRA inspected	
ERONDELLE			No 1 Section on dismounted parade. Lieut A.D.Evans posted to D.A.C. (No 1 Section) XIX Ammunition	
	28.		Officers Lt A D EVANS Ammunition Officer XIX posted to D.A.C. No 1 Section after Nd med. Church Parade by General W.B.R. Sandys C.M.G. XIX Corps. Inspected HQ Nos 1 + 2 Section completed column or position of ammunition. Draft of 5 Gunners re-inforcements arrived for the following – 4 for 33rd Brigade + 1 for 51st Brigade	
	29.		Examination of officers under rank of Major in D.A.C. on Gunnery + fitting of Harness. Also ammunition ranging – Signal training started. Capt T.H. Barrow returned.	
	30.		Draft of 6 drivers Gunners from re-inforcement camp arrived posted as follows :- 4 to 33rd Brigade, 1 to 45th Brigade + 1 to D.A.C. No 2 Section changed camp to other side of road in very wet weather. Refitting nearly completed	

WAR DIARY
or
INTELLIGENCE SUMMARY.

Army Form C. 2118.

Place	Date	Hour	Summary of Events and Information	Remarks and references to Appendices
ERONDELLES	1.5.18		Filled up No1 + 2 Sections with ammunition. Formed dump at ERONDELLES for Battns under Lt DAUGHTY	
			337/6A + 666A.X. Warning received that 8th D.Artillery will be leaving Lt Army Area on 2nd or 3rd inst.	
			PONTREMY station alternative.	
	2.5.18		S.A.A. Section moved back from line to SALEUX. Dump finished at ERONDELLE. Draft of 5 arrived from	
			Reinforcement camp, as follows 1 wheeler to 33rd Brigade and 4 How gunners 2 went to each Section (1+2 Sections)	
	3.5.18		Draft of 9 arrived from re-inforcement camp, as follows 5 arrived for 33rd Brigade, 3 drivers for 45th Brigade	
			1 S/Bdr + 2 drivers to No1 Section + 1 wheeler + 2 drivers to No. 2 Section.	
	4.5.18		Preparation for move to SALEUX	
ERONDELLE/SALOUEL	5.5.18		Advance party left for SALUEX at 6am. HQrs moved at 12 noon from starting point arriving 6.10pm	
			Both sections were open up + moved with Batteries. Billeted at SALOUEL. SAA section rejoined here.	
			16 Remounts arrived from ABBEVILLE	
	6.5.18		Advance party left for new area by train from SALUEX + arrived at FERE-EN-TARDEROIS on 7th inst.	
	7.5.18		HQrs moved for new area by train Both section moved with Batteries during 6th + 7th inst in small	
			parties. New Village is CUIRY-HOUSE.	
CUIRY-HOUSE	8.5.18		HQrs arrived at 6am + Sections joined up + billeted in same village. SAA section billeted at	
			SERINGES-ET-NESLES. Remount distribution to Sections.	

Army Form C. 2118.

WAR DIARY
or
INTELLIGENCE SUMMARY.
(Erase heading not required.)

Vol 42

Instructions regarding War Diaries and Intelligence Summaries are contained in F. S. Regs., Part II. and the Staff Manual respectively. Title pages will be prepared in manuscript.

Place	Date	Hour	Summary of Events and Information	Remarks and references to Appendices
Guiry-House	9.5.18		Horses at Divisional Hqrs doing Cavalry WOR returned also I.G.S. wgn from Division	
	10.5.18		S.A.A. Section moved to Mont-St-Martin. S.A.A. section completed with ammunition 11 cwt.	
			Notification received that this section would be controlled by divisional direct. Advance party left for new area.	
Guiry House Les Venteaux	11.5.18		H.Qrs 1 + 2 sections moved from Guiry-House tanned in Les Venteaux at 2.30 pm	
Les Venteaux	12.5.18		5th D.A. dumps started. QF wagons emptied also G.S. & Tart advance dump. 1096 A + 308 AX	
			396 BX all loads delivered to Battery positions by F.S. Majors. Lt. Ross Yc of 45" Brigade dumps 2nd in Shell Yc of 33rd Brigade dump. 2 in-bought Yc dump to supply both 33rd + 12" Brigade dumps.	
	13.5.18		Ammunition delivered to Batteries 1176 A 336 AX 396 BX night 12/13"	
			" " " 3462 A 984 AX 1084 BX " 13"/14"	
Les Grand Savarts	15.5.18		Moved to Les Grand Savarts. SAA section rejoined 4th section in same camp.	
			1606 A 464 AX 300 BX night 14"/15"	
	16.5.18		Ammunition delivered 2786 A 420 AX 916 BX night 15"/16"	
	17.5.18		" " 1519 A 385 AX 960 BX " 16"/17"	
	18.5.18		" " 160 A 56 AX " 17"/18"	

Army Form C. 2118.

WAR DIARY
or
INTELLIGENCE SUMMARY.
(Erase heading not required.)

Vol 47

Place	Date	Hour	Summary of Events and Information	Remarks and references to Appendices
LES GRAND SAPINS	19/5/18		Stock ammunition Dump for Infantry Brigade a/Pontavert cavalry with S.A.A. 250,000 Very Lights	
			5,1000 A.T.(M.G.) 99,840. Mobile reserve totals 760,000 S.A.A.	
LES GRAND SAPINS	20/5/18		2/Lt P.L. Nevitt relinquished duties of Assistant Adjutant and appointed A/8th T.M.B.y	
			2/Lt Mc Laughlin landed over 9th R.G.A. main dump and assumed duties of Asst Adjutant	
			2/Lt L. Jellinek took R over 8th R.G.A. main dump.	
			Ammunition delivered to Batteries night 19/20th ML	
do	21/5/18		" to 8th Div Wing 6TD6NY 60 Boxes S.A.A. M.G. = 62,400 Rnds.	
			" to Emergency Dumps 250,000 S.A.A. M.G. 1000 rifle, 3 inch	
do	22/5/18		" 200 Boxes Very lights 1" 6.25 th Infy Bde. Trench Mortar Bombs	
do	23/5/18		" 400 Rounds 3" Stokes T.M. Bombs	
			" 1000 " 1 inch Very Lights } to 24th Infy	
			" 600 Rifle Grenades No.23 } Brigade	
			" 134000 Rifle M.G. night 22/23	
			" 53,800 R.A.A.	
			" to Batteries night 22/23 168 A 48 AX	

Army Form C. 2118.

WAR DIARY
or
INTELLIGENCE SUMMARY.
(Erase heading not required.)

Vol IV Ref map

Instructions regarding War Diaries and Intelligence Summaries are contained in F. S. Regs., Part II. and the Staff Manual respectively. Title pages will be prepared in manuscript.

Place	Date	Hour	Summary of Events and Information	Remarks and references to Appendices
LES. GRAND SAYARTS	24/9/16	8th	Divisional Artillery School of Instruction opened, under the administration of the G.O. 5th D.A.C. Officer instructors { Lieut J.S. Harper R.G.A. – Gunnery Instructor / Lieut L.L. Eggleton R.G.A. – Signalling " / Capt A.E. Palmer & Lieut G.L. Learson R.G.A. joined from Base	
	25/9/16		Ammunition received 22 ppr 116	
			Capt A.E. Palmer met Brig – Genl R.A.	
			Capt A.E. Palmer baths 16.33 & Brig - Genl	
	26/9/16 4pm		Ammunition received 18 pdr 168 A + 108 AX	
			J Hooker to O.P.6. attd to 169th for reporting guns to 105th + 12th Bdes on the line	
	26/9/16			
	27/9/16 3am		Ammunition received 18 pdr 2579th 1116	
			3am Received orders to fill all vehicles of D.A.C. and 1st section 25th D.A.C.	
	9:30am		Despatch received 152 18 pdr wagons 2nd D.A.C. discharge by Batt. Jerusalem attached to 1st section 6th D.A.C.	
	1:30pm		One mounted Orderly per section called to report to H.Q. 6th Div Coy	
			Capt A.E. Palmer + Lieut G.L. 33rd + 45th Brigades RFA return to Base	

WAR DIARY or INTELLIGENCE SUMMARY

Army Form C. 2118.

(Erase heading not required.)

VOL XV   Ref. Map SOISSONS 1:100,000

Place	Date	Hour	Summary of Events and Information	Remarks and references to Appendices
LES GRANDS SAVARTS	24/5/18	2.0pm	8th D.A.C. march via route to BREUIL – via MONTIGNY – LES VENTEAU	
			1st Section 8th D.A.C. Rta to ROMAIN	
BREUIL VENDEUIL		5.0pm	8th D.A.C. marched to UNCHAIR.	
BREUIL VENDEUIL		2.30pm	S.A.A. Section marched – continued – to VENDEUIL	
ROMAIN VENDEUIL		2.30pm	No. 1 Section 8th D.A.C. joined 8th D.A.C. at UNCHAIR and immediately march'd to 2-7pm Q.F. Wagons and VENDEUIL as per order. March'd Lorry attach'd to them.	
			1-4.5 Q.F. Wagons from 6th D.A.C.	
LES GRANDS SAVARTS			Constitution of the 24 Sept 4/18pm Box Waistc. S.A. – Wounded 4.0pm 18pr. Brass R — " 6.6.13 " Brass C — "	
UNCHAIR GRUGNY		11.0pm	R.Q. D.A.C. & No.1 Section march'd to GRUGNY	
GRUGNY LHÉRY	28/5/18	3.12am	H.Q. D.A.C. & No 1 Sections march'd to LHÉRY via TRAMERY	
LHÉRY CHATILLON	28/5/18	2.0pm	H.Q. D.A.C. march'd .... to X roads to the S.S.E. of CHATILLON	
			Report cent. 8 D.A.C. heavy Sh.F day in CORBIZON	
CHATILLON CHAMBRECY	30/5/18	Afternoon	Orders received for 8 D.A.C. to proceed to CHAMBRECY (Chas G.S.Wagons) Casualties weight 28/29 — Drive atd — 66002 Gnr Rebeira J 8851 Dvr Jenkins G 20127 " Ronan S	

WAR DIARY or INTELLIGENCE SUMMARY

Army Form C. 2118.

Ref: Sheet SOISSONS 5.2
VOL. 42

Place	Date	Hour	Summary of Events and Information	Remarks and references to Appendices
VENDEUIL-CHATILLON	29/5/16	9 p.m.	No.1 Abstraction party arrived S.E of Rd at camp to made S.E of CHATILLON x Road	
LHERY CHAMBRECY		10.45 pm	No.2 Section 8th D.H's moved off and camped N of close to 'CHAMBRECY' - a little N of VILLE-EN-TARDENOIS	
		1.30 pm	No 1-2 Section "B" Echelon marched to LE NEUVILLE AUX LARRIS	
		2. pm	H.Q. 87 D.A.C, G.S. Wagons of 1st section and 1st section 25th D.A.C. moved off with orders to camp about the wood "PORT" of MAREUIL LE PORT	
CHATILLON MAREUIL LE PORT				
CHAMBRECY BOUJACOURT		5.15 pm	1st section 8th D.H's marched to BOUJACOURT (close to 18" Echelon)	
ditto		6.30 pm	No 2 section (close "B" Echelon) marched to camp - South of BOUJACOURT	
			on track below M. Plan CHAMPLAT	
MAREUIL LE PORT LA GRANDE FOSSE	30/5/16		H.Q. D.H.C. marched under orders to LA GRANDE FOSSE having their by the 1st section of the D.H.C and 5-18pr Q.F. wagons and all ZZ wagons of 1st section	
BOUJACOURT NANTEUIL	30/6/16		13 - 18pdr Q.F. wagons and 6 - 4.5 Q.F. Wagons of the 2nd section attached to 19th D.A.C. (19th Rear heavy Column were the first to arrive attached to this front South of NANTEUIL	
CHATILLON MAREUIL LE PORT IGNY-LE-TARD		4 pm	No 1 Section 25 D.H.C. rejoined 25 D.H.C. at IGNY-LE-TARD (Refer CARLON SH 50)	
			Car letter arrived to Bois DE BOURSAULT exchange at ? map sheet 50	
			} 13 en BOURSAULT Ref CHALONS map sheet 50	

Army Form C. 2118.

WAR DIARY
or
INTELLIGENCE SUMMARY. [Grp. Hosp. CHALONS 57]
(Erase heading not required.)

VOL 42

Place	Date	Hour	Summary of Events and Information	Remarks and references to Appendices
LES GRANDES LOGES ETANG DE RUSSON	2/5/16	10.0 am	HQ DDS told lorries and men parties of Adv parties marked to camp about 300 yds behind of Hen Camp of ETANG DE TOSSON 2½ m ST MARTIN d'ABLIS though "Y" on BROGNY — VILLERS-AU-BOIS.	
BOIS DE BOURGALT ETANG DE RUSSON		12.45 pm	EPA lorries marched to approx DP1 in Camp ETANG DE RUSSON	
		4.0 pm	Lorries received total 6.2 tractors (later attached to g.H.DP6) were camped at posts Rdvs ts if the fired G in CORMOVENT Announced from night to relieve men 16.835 Horses AxAx 32 aux 10 X	

(signature) Capt RPC
Capt Ord D.D.S

8 D Aus Ck
Army Form C. 2118.
Vol 4 3

WAR DIARY
INTELLIGENCE SUMMARY
(Erase heading not required.)

Ref map CHALONS 50

Place	Date	Hour	Summary of Events and Information	Remarks and references to Appendices
ETANG DE RUSSON	1/6/18	12 noon	"A" Echelon to be conveyed to Army between Railway Line Cornus - Finel about 1/2 m.	
STANG DE RUSSON	10/6/18	9.30 AM	D.A.C. less DAVIDSON Detachment (Parties of two A.T. officers + 9 + 2 ORs) marched in two echelons to LE MESNIL arriving via GIVRY - SOUILLERS - Cross Roads Just N.W. of	
LE MESNIL	24/6	9 AM	VENTUS to arrive G at CONGEST at meeting about 400 men N. of Tk. Y. in Sh. FERTEU	
			It is presumed parties to Givers (Brieau supposed Reed about 58° Sqs 13 cm	
		11.00 am	Orders received that a Group of 2 Batteries of 2 15pdr + 3 Gun Battalion and 1.4.5	
			Howz Battery from 9th D.A.C. Nos 12-5ton G.S. Wagons + 6. 4.5 G.S. Wagons under command of Lieut L.G. Aulkir RPA Formed "A" Echelon D.A.C. LEE WARNERS Group.	
			4. 8pr G.S. Wagons, 11 G.S. Wagons 4.5 showz, 1 G.S. Wagon Technical Stores formed "B"	
			Echelon under Command of Lieut Anton RPA.	
		3/6 pm	41 N.C.Os + men posted from 5th to 45th Bty	to form
			48 NCO + men " " " 32nd Bty	
			21 NCOs + men " " TM: to 45th Bty	LEE WARNERS Group
			12 NCOs + men " " TM: to 33rd Bty	

Officers posted to Battery from D.A.C. Lieuts S.T. BOORMAN, E GILBERT, A CROPPER
Lieut DUNNET; BIBBY, LATIMER + RLG

WAR DIARY or INTELLIGENCE SUMMARY

Army Form C. 2118.

VOL 43   N° of B'de CHALONS 59

Place	Date	Hour	Summary of Events and Information	Remarks and references to Appendices
LE MESNIL	1/6/18	9pm	Lieut Sutton of DAC "A" Echelon plus detachment of 33rd & 5th Bdes ammn wagons appeared	
			N°8 Brigade respectively marching via VAUCIENNES — MOUSSY — GRAVES	
do	2/6/18	8.10am	1 Officer & 57 O.Rs Divnl Employment Coy arrived & temporarily attached garrison	
			posted to Brigades	
do		2.45pm	D.A.C. less LEE WARNERS Section moved to new wagon lines — marching thro' LE GRANDANT	
			SOUILLY — GIVRY — DAC bivouacking at South node 300 yds N.E. of the N—m	
			RUSSON on ETG de RUSSON	
		3.10pm	LEE WARNERS Section arrived & new wagon lines marching as per DAC and	
			bivouacking about 800 yds N.E. the R— in ETG de RUSSON	
ETG de RUSSON	4/6/18 11 noon		DAVIDSON'S detachment reported DAC at ETG de RUSSON	
do	5/6/18	2 pm	Col. F.W. BOTELIER DSO R.F.A. forwarded to Lieut Colonel SICK. Capt. T.H. DAVISON R.F.A.	
do	5/6/18	9 am	Dismounted Inspection parade by OC RA IX Corps	temporarily commanding D.A.C.
do		9.30am	Lieut L. JELLINCK R.F.A. posted to 40th Bde	
do	6/6/18	11 am	A.S.B.908 Colonel J. HOLMES SAA & Lorry 8th D.A.C. tried by F.G.C.M. for absence without leave	
do	7/6/18	6.30pm	D.A. Sports held in open space just N.E. the 2 St in ETG de RUSSON	

Army Form C. 2118.

WAR DIARY
or
INTELLIGENCE SUMMARY.
(Erase heading not required.)

Army HeadQrs. CHALON S.O. ARCIS

VOL 43

Place	Date	Hour	Summary of Events and Information	Remarks and references to Appendices
Etg du POISSON	9/6/18	10.45am	A.P.O. bus LEE WARNER'S Section marched via GIVRY - LOISY - GRAVELLE - DANNES - BROUSSY LE GRAND to CONNANTRE bivouacking in the woods near the CHATEAU E. of the E in CONNANTRE	
		11.45am	LEE WARNER'S Section marched and bivouacked as above	
CONNANTRE	10/6/18	5.0 pm	Capt. HOSNELLINGS RFA reported from 5th Bde. RHA and posted to command No 2 Section Capt. J.L. HUGINTON RFA reported from fuire Army Depot of Instruction and attached to No 2 Section	
"	11/6/18	9.00 am	Orders received for LEE-WARNER'S GROUP to dispatch forthwith and open respective units.	
"		2.0 pm	LEE WARNER'S Section departed B.H.S.	
"	12/6/18	—	Orders received that B.H.S. line CAR Section received march to SOMMESOUS and its extension for a destination in the ENGLISH front.	
"	13/6/18	3.45 pm	No 1 Section marched to SOMMESOUS via FERE-EN-CHAMPENOISE arriving at 8 pm	
"		10.0 pm	No.2 Gp B.H.S. " " " " " " L. am 13/6/18	
"	13/6/18	2 am	Wagon S.A.A., Amn. Section (less 6 GS wagon and 22 QF Wagon entrained. Lom Eff SOMMESOUS 6 am, arriving at PONT REMY 4 am 14/6/18.	
			Amn 1 Section 1. G.S. Wagon and 6 QF Wagons entrained with 83rd Batty RFA at 10. am. Train leaving at 3 pm. — 1 G.S. Wagon and 6 QF Wagons entrained entrained with 364 Batty at 3 pm leaving at 6 pm — 1 G.S. Wagon and 5 QF Wagons entrained with 64th Batty at 6 pm leaving at 10 pm	

Army Form C. 2118.

WAR DIARY
or
INTELLIGENCE SUMMARY.
(Erase heading not required.)

Ref Major ARCIS
& FRANCE 62E

VOL 43

Instructions regarding War Diaries and Intelligence Summaries are contained in F. S. Regs., Part II. and the Staff Manual respectively. Title pages will be prepared in manuscript.

Place	Date	Hour	Summary of Events and Information	Remarks and references to Appendices
CONNANTRE	11/6/18	6.0pm	No 2 Section marched to SOMMESOUS via FERE-en-CHAMPENOISE arriving at 9.0 pm.	
		10.0pm	No 1 Section (11.00 H. 6.L Wagons and 23 Q.F. Wagons entrained with 46 Wagons R.Div Stay) leaving at 2 a.m. 14th. —1 QF wagon and 6 Q.F. Wagons entrained with 1st Batty QFPK Train leaving	
			at 6. a.m. 14th — 1 QF " " " 3rd " " " 6 a.m. "	
			at 10 am 14th — 1 QS " " " " " " " 10 am 14th "	
			at 2 pm 14th — 1 QS " " 5 " " marched to SEZANNE entraining & starting and	
			entrained with 54th Batty QFPK at 5.0pm train leaving 9 am 14th	
"	12/6/18 11.30pm		1/2 S.A.A Section marched to FERE CHAMPENOISE arriving at 12.45am entrained at 1.18 am 13th Train leaving at 5.18 am 13th	
"	13/6/18 10.30am		1/2 SAA Section marched to FERE CHAMPENOISE arriving at 5.45 a.m. entrained at 6.19am Train leaving at 10.19 am.	
	14-15/6/18		H.Q. D.T.C and Sections arrived at detraining stations — PONT-REMY — LONGPRE — HANGEST, and marched to ALLERY, where D.A.C Rallied.	
ALLERY	18/6/18	11.30pm	Orders received that Q.F. Wagon teams in DAC would be reduced from 6 to 4. Lorry teams from 3 to 2. Spare horses in Sec 1 + 2 Sections from 40 to 64, and dumped that spare horses from 90 to 82.	
"		11.30pm	46 trucks saddlery owing to new establishments sent to Ordnance Depot MARGUERITE by rail.	
	19/6/18	9.0am	21 E.S Wagons forwarded to Reinforcement Camps (2/2 at Arvis /c.) to fit equipments for 8th Div Arty. LIERCOURT	

Army Form C. 2118.

WAR DIARY
or
INTELLIGENCE SUMMARY.

(Erase heading not required.)

Instructions regarding War Diaries and Intelligence Summaries are contained in F. S. Regs., Part II. and the Staff Manual respectively. Title pages will be prepared in manuscript.

1st/4th Essex FRANCE 62 E
Sheets 14v.16 1/100,000

VOL 43

Place	Date	Hour	Summary of Events and Information	Remarks and references to Appendices
ALLERY	19/6/18	2.30pm	Lt/Driver G.F. Simmons Reinforcements arrived for RFA { 1 Sergt., 1 Corpl., 1 Dvr.	
	19/6/18	" 3pm	Lieut. W.H.G. LONDON RFA. joined from 4th Army Reinforcement Camp. Posted to No 2 Section.	
			Lieut. A.G.J. WHITBY RFA " " " " " " " No 1 "	
			2/Lieut T.M. OGILVIE RFA " " " " " " " No 1 "	
			2/Lieut T. MALTBY RFA " " " " " " " S.A.A "	
	22/6/18		2/Lieut W.H. PYE RFA HQ. section posted to 408 Bde. RFA	
			2/Lieut W.R. STOWE RFA " " " " " " " "	
			2/Lieut L.E.L. HEMPEL RFA HQ. " " " " " 33rd "	
ALLERY	2/6/18	10.0pm	Ercas Pioneer Coy. 1st Divn. only arrived march to GAMACHES AREA.	
	23/6/18	6.0am	D.A.C. marched via DISEMONT - BOUTTEN COURT - GAMACHES Billeting in BEAUCHAMPS	
BEAUCHAMPS	24/6/18	10.30am	60 N.C.Os & men of the 211th Res. Employment Company, attached D.A.C. returned to their unit.	
"	25/6/18	2.30pm	Inspection of 8th D.A.C. Ammunition by R.S.M. 4th Army in D.A.C. lines	
"	26/6/18	9.0pm	8th D.A.C. Signalling Class Commenced under Lieut. C.L. DAWSON RFA	
			No 64958 Sergt. E. WEATHERITT No 2 Section } Awarded the Military Cross for gallantry and devotion to duty between the AISNE and the MARNE	
			No 8851 " C.T. TOMPKINS " " " } from 29th May to 2 June, 1918. Auth. 8th D.R.O. No 211 of 29/6/18	
	28/6/18		Captain T.H. DAVISON RFA HQ DAC	
			2/Lieut T. MOSS RFA - No 2 Section } Awarded the MILITARY CROSS for Gallantry and devotion	
			2/Lieut L. JELLINEK RFA - (CO/Wh) Section } to duty between the AISNE and the MARNE from 27th May	
				to 2nd June 1918. Auth 8th D.R.O. No 219 of 28/6/18
	30/6/18	6.0pm	Lieut. A.G.J. WHITBY RFA No. 2 Section, posted to 49th Divn.	

(signed) M. Manion
Capt. RFA
Comdg. 8th Divn. Ammn. Column

Army Form C. 2118.

8 D Aus Col
VOL 44

WAR DIARY
or
INTELLIGENCE SUMMARY.
(Erase heading not required.)

Instructions regarding War Diaries and Intelligence Summaries are contained in F. S. Regs., Part II. and the Staff Manual respectively. Title pages will be prepared in manuscript.

Place	Date	Hour	Summary of Events and Information	Remarks and references to Appendices
BEAUCHAMPS	4/4/18	—	2. O.R. Reinforcements joined from 4th Army Reinforcement Camp.	
"	5/4/18	—	4 Officers joined from 4th Army Reinforcement Camp, viz: Lieuts R. W. WHITE, V. B. WIGGLESWORTH, E. CRANMER, A. J. SKELTON.	
"	6/4/18	—	Lieut A. J. SKELTON posted to 45th Brigade R.F.A. Lieut E. CRANMER " " 33rd " "	
"	7/4/18	—	49 N.C.O.s & men joined from 4th Army Reinforcement Camp.	
"	9/4/18	—	Lieut T. M. OGILVIE R.F.A. posted to C/293 Brigade A.F.A.	
"	10/4/18	—	Lieut W. H. P. LANDON R.F.A. " " " 3rd Division. 100 Remounts arrived from Remount Depot DIEPPE and distributed to Brigades as follows. 14 Riders 61.L.D. to 33rd Brigade. 21.L.D. to 45th Bde. 1 Rider to 8th D.A.C.	
"	13/4/18	—	8 L Divisional Horse Show on wheel 8th D.A.C. competed.	
"	14/4/18	—	Lieut (acting) D. G. W. DAVIES - Adjutant 8th D.A.C. struck off strength 8th D.A.C. from 29.6.18. Lieut J. G. DOUGHTY R.F.A. assumed duties of acting Adjutant.	
"	15/4/18	2.30pm	Address by — G. O. C, 8th Division to all R.A. Officers 8th Division.	
"	15/4/18	—	114 O.R.s reinforcements joined from 4th Army Reinforcement Camps and distributed as follows: 45 to 33rd Bde, 39 to 45th Bde. 26 to 8 Divn Arty Signal School, 5 Ord to 8th D.A.C.	
"	16/4/18	—	Inspection by C.R.A. 8th Divn Arty of NCOs+men at Divn Arty Signal School & Horses of teams & officers.	

Army Form C. 2118.

WAR DIARY
or
INTELLIGENCE SUMMARY.
(Erase heading not required.)

Ref. maps
ABBEVILLE } 1/100,000
LENS

VOL 44

Instructions regarding War Diaries and Intelligence Summaries are contained in F.S. Regs., Part II. and the Staff Manual respectively. Title pages will be prepared in manuscript.

Place	Date	Hour	Summary of Events and Information	Remarks and references to Appendices
BEAUCHAMPS	17/4/18	10 p.m.	N.Q. 3rd D.A.C. entrained GAMACHES.	
		11.56 p.m.	No 2 Section (less 2 Lt. G.S.wagon) entrained GAMACHES	
		8.2 p.m.	No 1 " " No. Q.F. " " EV.	
		11.2 p.m.	No 1 Section - 1 G.S. Wagon, + Q.F. wagon " " with 32nd Batty R.F.A.	
	18/4/18	2.56 a.m.	No 2 " ditto " GAMACHES " 1st Batty R.F.A.	
		5.56 a.m.	No 2 " ditto " " " 3rd " "	
		8.36 a.m.	No 2 " ditto " " " 5th " "	
		11.36 a.m.	No 2 " ditto " " " 54th " "	
		2.2 a.m.	No 1 " ditto " EV " 33rd " "	
		5.22 a.m.	No 1 " ditto " " " 55th " "	
		8.2 a.m.	No 1 " ditto " " " 36th " "	
LIGNY-ST.FLOCHEL	19/4/18	—	N.Q. D.A.C. + No 2 Section detrained at intervals at LIGNY-ST. FLOCHEL and marched to BLEUE and Camping Ground, S.W. end of OURTON	
BRYAS	"	—	No 1 Section detrained at intervals at BRYAS and marched to Camping Ground, S.W. end of OURTON.	
BEAUCHAMPS	20/4/18	1 a.m.	Half D.A.C. Section entrained FEUQUIERES detrained same day at PERNES.	
		10.22	" " " " EV " " " SAVY	
	29/4/18	—	Half D.A.C. Section march from PERNES to BARLIN and camped.	
			" " " SAVY to BLACKPOOL SIDING camping at F.11.c.45.90. (By hosp 57 H.S.)	

Army Form C. 2118.

WAR DIARY
or
INTELLIGENCE SUMMARY.
(Erase heading not required.)

Vol 44

Place	Date	Hour	Summary of Events and Information	Remarks and references to Appendices
OURTON	22/4/18	6.30 am	Orders received to relieve 72nd Bde. Billeting party of 3 officers & 16 O.Rs. proceeded by Lorry to 72 Bde over Bellets Brunhaut from 85 Bde.	
		10.30 am	Dumps taken over. LA TARGETTE DUMP A.8.a.8.9. Ref map sheet 51B. N.W. BRANDON DUMP F.10.c.0.5. " " 51 C. N.E.	
"	23/4/18	9.00 am	Officer i/c DUMPS Lieut O.P.E.A.B. HILL RFA, No1 Section 84 D.A.C. O.P.C. (Lieut. E.A.P. Sutton) march to new billets M.T. ST ELOY Ref map sheet 51 C N.E. HQrs billeting at F.8.b.5.6., No1 Section F.8.b.4.3., No2 Section F.8.b.4.6. marching via GAUCHIN-LEGAL - CHAGLAIN - L'ABBE - MT ST ELOY.	
BARLIN	23/4/18	-	No.1 D.A.P. Section camped at BARLIN.	
MT ST ELOY	23/4/18	-	Lieut F.W. HEAL R.F.A. & M. COUNSELL R.F.A. joined from 1st Army Reinforcement Camp	
	24/4/18	-	Lieut S.H. HARPER R.F.A, joined from R.O.N. 16 R.A. Base Depot	
	24/4/18	-	D.A.P. Section moved to new Camp F.9.a. 45.30. Ref map sheet 51C N.E.	
	26/4/18	-	Lieut R.B. MINTO R.F.A.; Lieut E.H. BECKET R.F.A. joined from 1st Army Reinforcement Camp	
	26/4/18		Lieut T. MALTBY R.F.A. posted to 33rd Brigade R.F.A.; Lieut G.L. DAWSON R.F.A. posted to 45th Brigade R.F.A.	
	28/4/18		Capt (Rev) EARDLEY WILMOT. H.Y. attached D.A.C. wounded & admitted to C.C.S.	

Army Form C. 2118.

WAR DIARY
or
INTELLIGENCE SUMMARY.

(Erase heading not required.)

VOL 44

Place	Date	Hour	Summary of Events and Information	Remarks and references to Appendices
MT ST ELOY	28/4/18	10 pm	Capt D.G.W DAVIES RFA (Adjutant) rejoined D.A.C.	
	29/4/18	—	Lieut H. WALKER posted to 8th Bgde French Mortar Brigade.	
	30/4/18	—	orders to provide 1 N.C.O + 2 men per detachment to man 3 Anti-Tank Guns.	

(signed) Major RFA
Capt 8th D.A.C.

WAR DIARY.
AUGUST 1918.
8th D.A.C.

WAR DIARY or **INTELLIGENCE SUMMARY.**
(Erase heading not required.)

Army Form C. 2118.

VOL 45

Place	Date	Hour	Summary of Events and Information	Remarks and references to Appendices
MONT ST ELOI (LENS 2 I.)	Aug 2		Reinforcements from 1st Army: 2 Sgts - 3 Corpls - 2 Bdrs - 15 signallers - 5 Drs	DGWD
			Lt A.C. LEACH joined from 1st Army Camp: posted to No:1 Section	DGWD
	3		Divisional DEFENCE TEST. "TEST ACTION" received 8.50 PM - "TEST STATION" received 9.23 PM	DGWD
	4		Lt B. ST J. STORRS joined from BASE: posted to No:2 Section	
	5		17 Remounts joined: 10 sold to 45th Bde, 7 to 33rd	
	6		2/Lt F.W. HEAL, No.2 Section, posted to 6th Div T.M.	DGWD
	7		a/Capt LAMBERT joined from 3rd Cav.Div.; posted to command No.1 Section; brought 2 chargers	DGWD
	8		H.M. the KING visited VIII Corps area. 200 mm D.A.C. paraded at 2.45 on road by which he passed	DGWD
	9		9 OR joined from 1st Army Camp: 6 posted to 33rd Bde	DGWD
	10		Col. F.W. BOTELER D.S.O. returned to 8th D.A.	DGWD
	11		Lt C.C. FAILES and 2/Lt L.C. ROWLES joined from 33rd Bde.	DGWD
	12		Lt. CC FAILES posted to No.2 section but in charge of Anti Tank Guns & therefore not for duty in DAC	DGWD
			2/Lt L.C. ROWLES posted to No.1 section	
			Lt R.S. LEWIS posted to 33rd Bde from SAA Section. Lt B. ST J. STORRS posted to 45th Bde from No.2 Section	
	13		a/Capt A.S. MELLING posted to SAA Section but remaining attached to No.2 section	DGWD
			a/Major T.H. DAVISON M.C. posted to command No 2 Section, returned to command 8th D.A.C.	
	14		2/Lt C.H. HOPKINS joined from 33rd Bde; posted to No:2 Section	DGWD
			Lt FAILES i/c Anti Tank Detachments became detached from No 2	
			8th Div Eliminating sports held	
			a/Capt A.S. MELLING reposted to No 2 Section	DGWD

Army Form C. 2118.

WAR DIARY
or
INTELLIGENCE SUMMARY.
(Erase heading not required.)

Instructions regarding War Diaries and Intelligence Summaries are contained in F. S. Regs., Part II. and the Staff Manual respectively. Title pages will be prepared in manuscript.

Place	Date	Hour	Summary of Events and Information	Remarks and references to Appendices
Mont St Eloi	Aug 16		1 Sgt 3 Gnrs, 4 Sigrs, 3 Drvs joined from 1st Army Reinforcement Camp. 4 horses to 33rd Bde RFA	DGWD
			4 - 45th - DAC	DGWD
	17		A.T. Tank (15 pdr) guns replaced by 18 pdrs by nos 1 & 2 sections	DGWD
	18		13 P.B. category men joined from Base for water Duty. 5 horses to 33rd & 45th Bdes RFA	DGWD
			2 - 3 - DAC	
	19		Lt C. Stuart R.F.A. joined from 9/6 Sup N.I.; attached to SAA section	DGWD
	20		2/Lt R.W. White SAA section attached DAC H.Q. as Asst A.V.F.	DGWD
	21			
	22		Lt C.C. Failes left DAC for two months in England	DGWD
	23		21 O.R. joined from 1st Army Reinforcement Camp. Postings - 33rd Bde 3 Gnrs 5 Drvrs	DGWD
			45th - 2 4	
			T.M. 4 3	
	24		VIII Corps Horse Show. DAC won 3 Firsts and 2 Thirds	DGWD
	25		Lt C. Stuart to hospital wounded. Lt A. Cliffach (M01) posted to 45th Bde - 6 Gnrs killed HSF & S.T. Mobile	DGWD
			Lt A. Ross - sick - 2/Lt R.B. Minto (M02) - 33rd - 9 - killed - 92 - -	DGWD
	26		NCO + 16 men left to collect remounts. H.V. Shells caused Gasualties Mo2section 4 killed 2 wounded to hospital	DGWD
	27		25 Recruits (14 L.D. + 11 Muleteers) joined from Depôt. 2/Lt Wigglesworth to Corps Signalling Course	DGWD
	29		NCO + 16 men from Base. 5 from 1st Army Reinforcement Camp	DGWD
	30		Timber Y'd A.R.P. A20 d 62 Shwt - 51 B taken over from 51st Div. Lt C. Stuart rejoined from hospital	DGWD
			Lt Gray to 277 Army Bde R.F.A. placed in charge	DGWD

J. Davidson Major
Commdg 8th DAC
31.8.16

WAR DIARY or INTELLIGENCE SUMMARY

Army Form C. 2118.

8 D Am Col

VOL 46

Place	Date Sept	Hour	Summary of Events and Information	Remarks and references to Appendices
MONT ST ELOI	2		Exchange of W.O. - BSM Hillyard, S.A.A section to 1st Bde; BSM Goodman to S.A.A section	DGWD
(LENS 2 I)	3		No IV section new and on Anti-Tank gun for Right Group — 2 BSM's joined from Base - attached	DGWD
	4		Capt F.W. Buckley R.F.A. joined from Base	DGWD
	5		2/Lt H.D. Scott joined from Base, posted No 2 Section — BSM Milchard (attached) posted to 55th Bde BAC	DGWD
			Capt F.W. Buckley posted to 33rd Bde — 17 Reinforcements disposal:- 45th Bde — 9 Gnrs	
			33 — 4	
			HQ RA — 1 Driver	
			8th DAC — 3 Gnrs	
	6		Sgt Bath, No 1 Section and Sgt Denmark, No 2 Section attached to BQMS's to 49th DAC & 48th BAC	DGWD
	8		66 Remounts joined from Fruges Remount Dept	DGWD
	9		1 Corp & 3 Shoeing Smiths joined for 1st Army Reinforcement Camp	DGWD
	11		2 Shoeing Smiths joined from 42 BAC	DGWD
	13		Draft of 20 OR from 1st Army Reinforcement Camp. Disposal:- 45th Bde — 6	DGWD
			33rd Bde — 7	DGWD
			8th DAC — 7	
	14		No 1 Section moved from huts at St Eloi to camp at A 2 d 5.5 (Sheet 51 B N.W.)	DGWD
	15		2/Lt J.A.A. Taylor joined from Base; posted to No 2 Section	DGWD
			A/BQMS Mallison (attached) posted to 55th Bde BAC	DGWD

Army Form C. 2118.

WAR DIARY
or
INTELLIGENCE SUMMARY.
(Erase heading not required.)

Instructions regarding War Diaries and Intelligence
Summaries are contained in F. S. Regs., Part II.
and the Staff Manual respectively. Title pages
will be prepared in manuscript.

Place	Date	Hour	Summary of Events and Information	Remarks and references to Appendices
Mont St Eloi	Sept 16		Capt. R. Skelton joined from 33rd Bde; attached HQ DAC	DGwD
			Capt Herold joined from Base & proceeded to 33rd Bde.	DGwD
	17th		2/Lt Milsom joined from Base attached No.1 section	DGwD
			Test run over B A/C tactful detachment - Transp. (No 2 section)	DGwD
	18th		Nos. 1 & 2 section keep one subsection each to take part in tactical scheme with 2 Bdes in	PGwD
	(19)		Subsect joined from Base; posted to 45 Bde. No 2 section him at no subsection in marching order	
	20		2/Lt Scott No 2 subsec. posted to 3rd Bde BSM Keegan posted to No 2 section for 4 Div	DGwD
			2/Lt Milsom posted to 5th	
			S.A.A. section him at ord subsection in marching order	
	22		1 gunner killed by shell in No 2 section lines; (1) horse wounded	DGwD
	24		S.O.R. joined from 1st Army Reinforcement Camp	DGwD
	25		8 O.R. & posted 45th Bde	
	26		1 NCO wounded; also 10 OD &, horses lost in SAA section lines	DGwD
	27			
	28		2/Lt White left in charge of party to collect remounts from Fruges	DGwD
	30		27 Remounts joined from Fruges; sent to the unit	DGwD

C. Blanquiere Major
Comdg 8th DAC
RFA.

8 DAC Cdn
Vol. 47 DUPLICATE   Army Form C. 2118.

WAR DIARY
or
INTELLIGENCE SUMMARY.
(Erase heading not required.)

WO 47

Place	Date Oct 1918	Hour	Summary of Events and Information	Remarks and references to Appendices
Mont St. Eloi	1			
	2		LA TARGETTE A.R.P. handed over to 20th Div'n - Lt. Ross and party now look over MAIN Dump at GIY.C (Sheet 51.b) from 51st Div'n	DGWD
	3		8th D.A.C. moved from Mont St Eloi to camp at MADAGASCAR CORNER vacated by 51st Div'n Amm. Col.	DGWD
Lens Map 1/100,000	4		TIMBER Yd Dump handed over to VIII Corps. New ARP at ROCLINCOURT opened	DGWD
	5		Lt MILLER and party of 30 Labour Batt's now opened CAM Dump at ST LAURENT BLANGY	DGWD
	6		Considerable work in clearing MAIN Dump & filling CAM Dumps	DGWD
	7			
	8		MAIN Dump closed for issue of Ammunition, handed over to Corps	DGWD
	9			
	10		New ARP opened at FAMPOUX H18c 9.6. Also dump established at I21.b. SW. q. PLOUVAIN Capt. R. SKELTON left 8th DAC & posted to R.A. training camp at Midrands near DIEPPE 8th D.A.C. moved from MADAGASCAR CORNER to MUSKETRY VALLEY in H13.6	DGWD
	11			DGWD
	12		Personnel of T.M. Batteries joined for duty X/6B5 to No.1 Section Y/6B5 to " 2 "	DGWD
	13		HQ, No.1 Section moved to C28.b.2.2 on main FRESNES – VITRY Rd No 2 " " " " IZEL Forward ARPs established at C28.b.2.2 ("A" dump) and IZEL ("B" dump) CRASH Dump FAMPOUX (H18.c.9.6) – PLOUVAIN – CAM Dumps emptied & closed ROCLINCOURT ARP handed over to VIII Corps. Every available man of this unit engaged in emptying back area dumps and old Battery positions.	DGWD

Ammunition issued to Batteries for period Oct 1st – Oct 10th :-
A — 15,986
AX — 10,741
BX — 5,696

Army Form C. 2118.

WAR DIARY
or
INTELLIGENCE SUMMARY.
(Erase heading not required.)

Instructions regarding War Diaries and Intelligence Summaries are contained in F. S. Regs., Part II. and the Staff Manual respectively. Title pages will be prepared in manuscript.

Place	Date	Hour	Summary of Events and Information	Remarks and references to Appendices
	14		SAA section moved to PLOUVAIN Shelling of HQ by 1 section finished by enemy HV gun caused casualties — 1 Shoeing Smith and 1 Gunner wounded — 2 Chargers + 1 mule killed — 1 mule wounded	D&WD
	15		Reinforcements HQ + No 1. moved to C.28.c. South of FRESNES. 17 Drivers joined from 1st Army Reinforcement camp + posted as follows:— 9 to 33rd Bde — 4 to 45th Bde — 4 to DAC.	DGWD
	17		2 OR of No 1 section wounded	DGWD
VALENCIENNES MAP 1/100,000	18		HQ + SAA section moved from FRESNES - PLOUVAIN area to PLANQUES (Refer Map VALENCIENNES 1/100,000 2 A). No 2 section moved to AUBY. 2 new ARP's formed No 1 at Flg d'ESQUERCHIN No 2 - AUBY	DGWD
	19		No 1 section moved to BREBIERES — No 2. to ANHIERS No dump formed at ANHIERS	DGWD
	20		HQ + SAA section moved to CATTELET S.E. of FLINES. The Battalion of 4th section of 311 BAC collected at CATTELET. QF wagons of No 1, 2 sections moved to RACHES + MARCHIENNES respectively. A" echelon of section was entirely under RFA brigades action	DGWD
	21		QF wagons of No 2 moved to BRILLON + SARS et ROSIERES	DGWD
	22		HQ, SAA section, and the B echelon moved from CATTELET to SARS ET ROSIERES	DGWD

WAR DIARY or INTELLIGENCE SUMMARY

Army Form C. 2118.

Place	Date	Hour	Summary of Events and Information	Remarks and references to Appendices
	23		HQ and Bechelen moved to PONCHELET-VERCOGNE area (VALENCIENNES M? 1 D.9.5) 30 Remounts joined. 10 sent to 33rd Bde. 20 sent to 45th Bde. No 2 section about to 5 LD & 45th Bde. Lt B. St J. Storrs R.F.A. joined No 1 section at BOUVIGNIES. No 2 section moved to LA BRUYERE SW of ST AMAND	Dowd
	24		No 1 Section moved to SARS LES ROSIERES - Lt E.C. Miller left for AUSTRALIA and was struck off strength "B" echelon of 48th Bac joined this unit at VERCOGNE	Dowd
	25		Lt WRIGHT A.R.P. spent at PONCHELET - Dump at AMHIERS emptied and closed. No 2 section moved to station yd ST AMAND	Dowd
	26		2/Lt WIGGLESWORTH R.F.A. attached from No 1 section to No 2 section No 1 section sent 5 LD to 33rd Bde	Dowd
	27		No 2 section sent 15 LD & 45th Bde - No 1 section sent 10 LD to 33rd Bde 5 LD & 45th -	Dowd
	28		2 6" Trench Mortars on mobile carriers taken into action on outpost line. No 1 & 2 sections each detached team of mules & drivers for these 2 TM Guns	Dowd
	29		20 Gunners & 9 Drivers joined from 1st Army Reinforcement Camp & posted to Brigades 11 Gunners & arrived to 33rd Bde 9 - - 45 - 3 - - -	Dowd

Army Form C. 2118.

WAR DIARY
or
INTELLIGENCE SUMMARY.
(Erase heading not required.)

Instructions regarding War Diaries and Intelligence Summaries are contained in F.S. Regs., Part II. and the Staff Manual respectively. Title pages will be prepared in manuscript.

Place	Date	Hour	Summary of Events and Information	Remarks and references to Appendices
	30		HQ & Bachelors & Mr 1&2 sections moved to MILLON FOSSE area. Mobile dumps at PONCHELET Wood & reformed at Junction S. of NOUVEAU JEU NW of MILLON FOSSE village.	DGWD
			Reinforcements for Brigade to be supplied by 9th DAC.	
			Not yet No 2 Sub Gunners 5 7 Drivers 13 3 Signallers 1 Sergeants — 3 Cpls — 2 Bombardiers — 1	
			All except 3 sergeants duplicates	
	31		SAA section of Bachelor & 48th B.A.C. joined their unit at MILLON FOSSE. Major CASTELLAN attached to this HQ for instruction from 126 Army Brigade.	DGWD

			Ammunition issued to Batteries for period Oct 24th to Oct 30th:-
			         A — 7448
			         Ax — 8146
			         Bx — 5152	

C.D. Davidson, Major R.F.A.
Comdg 8th Bde 2nd Army
1.11.18

Army Form C. 2118.

8th D.A.C. WAR DIARY December 1918.

Vol 49 INTELLIGENCE SUMMARY.

(Erase heading not required.)

Place	Date	Hour	Summary of Events and Information	Remarks and references to Appendices
ANTOING	1/12/18		Training, Recreation, Educational Schemes.	
"	2/12/18			
"	3/12/18		Billeting parties sent to TOURNAI to reconnoitre billets. Training.	
"	4/12/18		Training, Recreation, Education	
"	5/12/18		D.A.C. marched from ANTOING to TOURNAI	
TOURNAI	6/12/18		Training, Recreation, Education Schemes.	
"	7/12/18		H.M. the King visited TOURNAI Guard of honour of 1914 N.C.O's + men. 35 N.C.O's men joined from 5th Army Reinforcement Camp	
"	8/12/18		Training, Recreation, Education	
"	9/12/18			
"	10/12/18		7 O.R's joined from Base. Major T.H. Dawson M.C. returned from leave. 2 Sergts, 1 Corpl, 80 O.R's posted to 33rd Brigade R.F.A. 6 O.R's posted to 45th Brigade R.F.A.	
"	11/12/18		2 Sergts + 1 Gunner joined from Base. posted to 33rd Bde R.F.A.	
"	12/12/18		2 Sergts posted from 33 Bde R.F.A	
"	13/12/18		22 O.R's joined from Reinforcement Camp 5th Army.	
"	14/12/18		Training, Recreation	

Army Form C. 2118.

WAR DIARY
or
INTELLIGENCE SUMMARY.
(Erase heading not required.)

Instructions regarding War Diaries and Intelligence Summaries are contained in F. S. Regs., Part II. and the Staff Manual respectively. Title pages will be prepared in manuscript.

Place	Date	Hour	Summary of Events and Information	Remarks and references to Appendices
TOURNAI	15/12/18		F.M. Rae attached to Section DAC for duty returns & discipline. Routine parties out proceed to LEUZE & BASSILLY.	
—	16/12/18		D.A.C. marches from TOURNAI to LEUZE en route for BASSILLY.	
LEUZE	17/12/18		D.A.C. marches from LEUZE to BASSILLY.	
BASSILLY	18.12.18 to 25/12/18		Training, Recreation & Education.	
—	26/12/18		Major T.H. Davison M.C. to hospital. Major V.E. Crichton from No 2 Section to HQ & Command Column. Lt O.P.E.H.B. Wile & 2/Lt T.A.A. Taylor to England as demobilized.	
—	27/12/18		Training, Recreation & Education.	
—	28/12/18 to 29/12/18			
—	30/12/18		Lt C. Stewart posted from S.A.A. Section to No 2 Section. 2/Lt S.H. Harper to Ordnance College. Whilst S.A.A. ammunition train & railway between BASSILLY & LESSINES caught fire, causing heavy explosion. 1 Gunner slightly wounded. S.A.A. Section moved to CROISETTE. Training, Recreation & Education	
—	31/12/18			

V. Crichton
Major F.A. (T.F.)
Comdg. 9th D.A.C.

SECRET.   Copy No. 27

8th DIVISIONAL ARTILLERY ORDER No. 96.

Ref. Map 37. 1/40,000.   3rd December 1918.

1. 45th Brigade R.F.A., will march under Brigade arrangements on 4th December from present area to the following destinations :-

    Brigade H.Q.,   O.36.d.7.8.
    1 Battery.   St. MAUR.
    1 Battery.   ERE.   The Prison.
    2 Batteries.   TOURNAI (Personnel and
                         Wagon Lines adjoining).

    Move to be completed by 13.00 hrs. 4th inst., No restrictions as to route.

2. 8th D.A.C., and T.M. Brigade will march on 5th December under orders of O.C., 8th D.A.C., from present area to the following destinations :-

    Headquarters.   TOURNAI (College des Jesuits)
                         (Wagon lines with No.1 Sec).

    Nos.1 & 2 Sections. TOURNAI (Field E. of TOURNAI -
                         BRUYELLE Road in O.36.a & b).
                         Personnel in Infirmerie).

    S.A.A., Section.   O.36.c & d. (N. of Railway).

    T.M. Brigade.   TOURNAI. (Infirmerie).

    Move to be completed by 11.30 hrs. 5th instant.

3. Degat and "No Claims" certificates will be obtained in triplicate, original being retained by units and 2 copies forwarded to this office by last D.R., 5th December.

    All billets and Wagon Lines will be left in a clean and sanitary condition.

4. Units billeted in the Infirmerie will ensure that the indoor latrines are not used. Doors of same will be securely closed and marked with notices "NOT TO BE USED".

5. Completion of move to be reported to this office without delay.

6. 45th Brigade and 8th D.A.C., to acknowledge.

                                               Monton
                                        Capt. for B.M.R.A.,
                                        8th Divisional Artillery.

Issued at 1900 hrs

Distribution:-
    Copy No. 1-5   45th Bde.R.F.A.   19. 25th Inf. Bde.
           6-10   D.A.C.(and D.T.M.O.,   20. Town Major, TOURNAI.
              11   33rd Bde.R.F.A.   21.   "   "   ANTOING.
              12   119th Army Bde.RFA.   22.   "   "   WEZ VELVAIN.
              13   8th Division "G".   23. D.A., Signals.
              14   8th Division "Q".   24. C.R.A.,
              15   III Corps R.A.,   25. B.M.
              16   8th Div. Train.   26. S.C.,
              17   D.A.D.O.S.,   27-28 War Diary.
              18   D.A.D.V.S.,   29. File.

SECRET

Amendment No. 1. to 8th Divisional Artillery
Order No. 97.

14th December 1918.

Table 'A' will be amended as follows :-

Page 1. (a) Opposite 8th D.A.H.Q., under 'starting point and time' delete 'Pont aux Pommes Bridge, TOURNAI 08.00,' and substitute 'To be detailed by O.C., 8th D.A.C.,'

(b) Under 'remarks' add 'Marches with and under orders of 8th D.A.C.',

Page 2. (a) Opposite 8th D.A.H.Q., under 'To' delete 'GHISLENGHIEN' and substitute 'ENGHIEN.'

(b) Opposite 33rd Brigade R.F.A., under 'To' delete 'LEUZE' and substitute 'PIPAIX.'

Page 3. Delete last line.

Captain R.A.,
for Brigade Major,
8th Divisional Artillery.

Distribution.- To all recipients of 8th D.A. Order No.97.

SECRET.   Copy No ...20...

8th. Divisional Artillery Order No. 97.

10th. December 1918.

1. The 8th. Division will move to the ENGHIEN - ATH Area, commencing on "G" day, which will not be before 16th. December 1918. "G" day will be notified later.

2. 33rd, 45th and 119th (Army) Brigades R.F.A. will march as part, and under orders, of 23rd, 25th and 24th. Infantry Brigade Groups respectively.
   8th. Divisional Ammunition Column and Trench Mortar Brigade will march as one unit under orders from this office.

3. Intermediate and final destinations will be as shewn on attached table "A". In the case of Artillery Brigades these are liable to alterations by Infantry Brigade Groups.

4. Billeting for intermediate area will be arranged by Brigades in conjunction with their respective Infantry Brigade Groups.
   Billets for Divisional Ammunition Column at LEUZE will be notified later.

5. 8th. D.A.C. will send 4 G.S.Wagons with teams and Drivers to report to 33rd. and 45th. Brigades R.F.A. Headquarters at 15.00 hours 12th. December. These wagons will be attached to Brigades for the march and until further orders, and will be inspected by C.R.A. prior to above attachment.

6. Degat, no claim, and cleanliness certificates will be obtained, in duplicate, at all villages on route to final destinations and forwarded to this office by first D.R. on "I" plus 1 day.

7. Reports to present Headquarters till 10.00 hours "H" day, then to ENGHIEN.

8. Acknowledge.

                                           Captain R.A.
                                           for Major R.A.
                              Brigade Major, 8th. Divisional Artillery.

Issued to Signals
at 17.00 hours.

Distribution -
Copy No. 1 to 33rd. Bde.R.F.A.   12. 8th. Div. Train.
         2   45th. Bde.R.F.A.   13. D.A.D.O.S.
         3   119th.(Army)Bde.R.F.A. 14. D.A.D.V.S.
         4   8th. D.A.C.   15. C.R.A.
         5   D.T.M.O.   16. B.M.
         6   III Corps R.A.   17. S.O.
         7   8th. Division "G".   18. D.A.Signals.
         8   8th. Division "Q".   19-20 War Diary.
         9   23rd. Inf. Bde.   21 File.
        10   24th. Inf. Bde.   22-23 Spare.
        11   25th. Inf. Bde.

Page 1.

TABLE "A", issued with 8th. D.A. Order No. 97, 10/12/18. "G" Day.

Unit.	From.	To.	Starting Point Route. and time.		Remarks.
33rd. Bde. R.F.A.	Stands fast.				Send on billeting party to LEUZE, as arranged with 23rd. Inf. Brigade.
45th. Bde. R.F.A.	TOURNAI Area.	LEUZE.			Advance billeting parties proceeds to LEUZE on G-1 day, and to MAFFLE on "G" day.
119th.(Army) Bde. R.F.A.	Stands fast.				Send on billeting party as arranged with 24th. Infantry Brigade Group.
6th. D.A.O. and Trench Mortars	TOURNAI.	LEUZE.	PONT AUX POMMES Bridge, TOURNAI, 08.05.		Advance billeting parties proceed on G-1 day. Further details later. They go on to BASILLY on "G" day.
8th.D.A.,H.Q.	TOURNAI.	LEUZE.	PONT AUX POMMES Bridge, TOURNAI, 08.00.		

Page 2

Table "A", 8th. D.A. Order No. 97, 10/12/18.   "H" Day.

Unit.	From.	To.	Starting Point and time.	Route.	Remarks.
33rd.Bde.R.F.A.	BLANDAIN.	LEUZE.	Orders from 23rd. Infantry Brigade.		Billeting party proceeds in advance to final destination.
45th.Bde.R.F.A.	LEUZE.	MAFFLE.	Orders from 25th. Infantry Brigade.		—do—
119th.(Army) Bde.R.F.A.	BLANDAIN.	CHAPELLE-LEUZE PIPAIX area.	Orders from 24th. Infantry Brigade.		—do—
8th.D.A.C. and Trench mortars.	LEUZE.	BASILIX.	Inn ½ mile E of LEUZE. 0805.		
8th.D.A.F.Q.	LEUZE.	CHISLENGHIEN.	Inn ½ mile E of LEUZE 08.00.		

Table "A", 8th D.A., Order No. 97, 10/12/18. Page 3. 'I' Day.

Unit.	From.	To.	Starting Point and Time.	Route.	Remarks.
33rd Bde.R.F.A.	LEUZE.	MAFFLE Area.	Orders from 23rd Infantry Brigade.		
45th Bde.R.F.A.	MAFFLE	MARCQ Area.	Orders from 25th Infantry Brigade.		
119 (A) Bde.RFA.	CHAPELLE-LEUZE-PIPAIX Area.	ATTRE GAGES MEVERGNIES	Orders from 24th Infantry Brigade.		
8th D.A.C., and Trench Mortars.	STAND FAST.				
8th D.A., H.Q.,	GHISLENGHIEN.	ENGHIEN	GHISLENGHIEN CHURCH. 08.00.		

Jan-May 1919

WAR DIARY 8th D.A.C. (?)
or
INTELLIGENCE SUMMARY.
(Erase heading not required.)

JANUARY 1919

Army Form C. 2118.

Vol 50.

Place	Date	Hour	Summary of Events and Information	Remarks and references to Appendices
BASSILLY	1/1/19		Trainings proceed	
	2/1/19		3 men to England for Demobilisation. 50 Reinforcements joined	
	3/1/19		Training Educational Scheme 3 men to England for Demobilisation	
	4/1/19		England for Demobilisation etc Training Educational Scheme	
	5/1/19		" "	
	6/1/19		6 Reinforcements joined	
	7/1/19		150 Indian joined from BASE	
	8/1/19		Training & Educational Scheme	
	9/1/19		" "	
	10/1/19		12 men to England for Demobilisation. Capt D.G.W. Davies regimen	
	11/1/19		Men have 4 reinforcements joined	
	12/1/19		Training & Education. 9 men to England for demobilisation	
	13/1/19		8 " "	
	14/1/19		7 " "	
	15/1/19		11 " "	

Army Form C. 2118.

WAR DIARY
or
INTELLIGENCE SUMMARY.
(Erase heading not required.)

Instructions regarding War Diaries and Intelligence Summaries are contained in F. S. Regs. Part II. and the Staff Manual respectively. Title pages will be prepared in manuscript.

Place	Date	Hour	Summary of Events and Information	Remarks and references to Appendices
BASSILLY.	16/1/19		Major V.E. CASTELLAN to 74th Div for Reserve Board. Major A.E.M. FINLAY posted from 8th Div as officer to command 8th D.A.C. t/c Wheeler	
	17/1/19		Started as III Corps Ammunition Officer	
	18/1/19		Training & Education	
	19/1/19			
	20/1/19		Major T.E. HFORD to H.Q. CHERBOURG Base	
	21/1/19		Leaving 3 hours to England for demobilisation	
	24/1/19		Training & Education	
	25/1/19		Capt. W.B.R. LAMBERT and 6 O.R's to England for demobilisation	
	26/1/19		Major V.E. CASTELLAN returned from Reserve Board. Lt. ROSS and 20 O.R's to England for demobilisation	
	27/1/19		Training & Education	
	28/1/19		16 hours to England for demobilisation	
	29/1/19		Training & Education	
	30/1/19			

Army v R.H.A.
A/Adjt. 8th D.A.C.
for O.C. 8th D.A.C.

8th D.A.C. WAR DIARY FEBRUARY 1919
INTELLIGENCE SUMMARY

Army Form C. 2118.

JR 51

Place	Date	Hour	Summary of Events and Information	Remarks and references to Appendices
BASSILLY	1/2/19		Training & Educational Scheme	
	2/2/19		— do —	
	3/2/19		— do — 5 men to England for demobilization	
	4/2/19		Training & Educational Scheme	
	5/2/19		— do — 8 men to England for demobilization	
	6/2/19		— do —	
	7/2/19		— do — } do	
	8/2/19		— do — } 8	
	9/2/19		— do — 5	
	10/2/19			
	11/2/19		Training & Educational Scheme	
	12/2/19		— do — 3 men to England for demobilization	
	13/2/19		— do —	
	14/2/19		— do — 13	
	15/2/19		Training & Educational Scheme	
	16/2/19		9 "Y" horses to ATH for vacation to England. 10 "Z" horses to	
	17/2/19		BRUSSELS for sale. 13 men to England for demobilization	
	18/2/19		Training & Educational Scheme	
	19/2/19			

Army Form C. 2118.

WAR DIARY
or
INTELLIGENCE SUMMARY.
(Erase heading not required.)

Instructions regarding War Diaries and Intelligence Summaries are contained in F. S. Regs., Part II. and the Staff Manual respectively. Title pages will be prepared in manuscript.

Place	Date	Hour	Summary of Events and Information	Remarks and references to Appendices
BASSILLY	20/2/19		Training & Educational Scheme	
	21/2/19		— do —	
	22/2/19		— do —	
	23/2/19		— do —	
	24/2/19		Training & Educational Scheme	
	25/2/19		— do —	
	26/2/19		— do —	
	27/2/19		— do — D.A.C.	
	28/2/19		Join 3rd D.A.C.	

7 men to England for demobilization
16 — do —
— do —
8 — do —
1 — do —

1 man to England for demobilization
Major V.E. CASTELLAN proceeded to

[signature]
for Major 3rd D.G.
Cmdg 8th D.A.C.

Army Form C. 2118.

WAR DIARY 8th D.A.C.

INTELLIGENCE SUMMARY.

MARCH 1919 M 5 2

Place	Date	Hour	Summary of Events and Information	Remarks and references to Appendices
CASSILY	1/3/19 to 9/3/19		Training, Education & Recreation.	
	10.3.19		Lt. C. Stewart proceeds to Courai Kino for Draft conducting duties. Young Educational Scheme	
	11.3.19		2 men to England for demobilisation	
	12.3.19		— " —	
	13.3.19		Training, Education & Recreation.	
	14.3.19			
	15.3.19		2/Lt. J. Paterson + 5 OR's to England for demobilisation. Young Educational Scheme	
	16.3.19			
	17.3.19		Lt. H. Walker rejoined from leave.	
	18.3.19 to 27.3.19		Training, Education & Recreation.	
	28.3.19		1 OR to England for demobilisation	
	29.3.19 to 31.3.19		Training, Education & Recreation.	

A.R.W.
Major
for Major Cmdg. R.F.A.
Comdg. 8th D.A.C.

8th Divisional Ammunition Column

WAR DIARY

INTELLIGENCE SUMMARY

(Erase heading not required.)

Army Form C. 2118.

April 1919.

Place	Date	Hour	Summary of Events and Information	Remarks and references to Appendices
Bavilly	1/4/19 – 3/4/19		Training, Education, & Recreation	
	4/4/19		" " "	
	5/4/19		3 men to England for demob.	
	8/4/19		" " "	
	10/4/19		Lt. Hopkins C.H. to 33rd Div. R.A. Training, Education & Recreation	
	11/4/19		Education & Recreation	
	12/4/19		1 Officer & 20 B. Ranks Personnel to 138 Indian Personnel to 19 Stationary Hospital, Calais, as escort for Z Kneudene. Education & Recreation	
	13/4/19 to 15/4/19		" " "	
	16/4/19		Capt J.G. Dutton R.G.A. R.T.O. Lieut R.T.A. to 146 Div. Army R.G.A. Reinforcement Camp Cologne. Education & Recreation	
	17/4/19 to 21/4/19		" " "	
	22/4/19		200 mules to Corps Collecting Camp Kebric. Training, Education & Recreation	
	23/4/19		92 mules to Corps Collecting Camp Kebric.	
	24/4/19		Lt Hopkins A.E. Councill I.S.R. to 119 Div. R.A.	
	25/4/19		" " "	
	25/4/19 to 29/4/19		Training, Education & Recreation	
	30/4/19		" " "	

A.R. Lindsay
Major R.A.
Comdg. 8 D.A.C.

Army Form C. 2118.

WAR DIARY 2nd Divisional Ammunition Column

INTELLIGENCE SUMMARY

May 1919.

(Erase heading not required.)

Place	Date	Hour	Summary of Events and Information	Remarks and references to Appendices
Boosing	1/5/19 to 10.5.19		Training, Education & Recreation	
	11.5.19 12.5.19		Capt J.L. Bibby to England for demob	
	to 28.5.19		Training, Education & Recreation	
	29.5.19		Lieut C. Wheeler to Eng. for demob	
	30.5.19 31.5.19		Training, Education & Recreation	
			Training.	

M. M. Dutch Major R.F.A.
Comdg 2nd D.A.C.

B.E.F.

8 DIV.

A.A. SECTION

1914 SEPT. to 1914 ~~NOV~~ DEC

War Diary — ANTI-[Aircraft] Det 1st Division

Box/136

War Diary of the 1st Anti Aircraft Detachment
8th Division

From date of formation 9.9.14
To 30th November 1914

Army Form C. 2118.

Sheet 1

WAR DIARY
or
INTELLIGENCE SUMMARY.
(Erase heading not required.) Anti Aircraft Detachment 8th Division

Hour, Date, Place	Summary of Events and Information	Remarks and References to Appendices
HILSEA 9/9/14	The detachment was formed at HILSEA BKS, COSHAM. Lieut Fryer and 3 NCO's RGA from No 4 Depôt RGA. 7 Gunners RGA from No 1 Depôt RGA. 7 Drivers RFA from 3A Res Bde RFA. 6 horses " " "	
HILSEA 11/9/14	The gun and wagon, ammunition and stores were sent direct from WOOLWICH. It was known that a 6.5 wagon would be part of the unit but not known when it would be handed over. — Mention of it was made in the only equipment detail available at HILSEA, and that it was to carry 2000 rounds of ammunition from rear. Service information was obtained that this would be obtained at the Ordnance base. The stores sent from WOOLWICH contained	

WAR DIARY
INTELLIGENCE SUMMARY.
(Erase heading not required.)

Army Form C. 2118.

Sheet 2

Hour, Date, Place	Summary of Events and Information	Remarks and References to Appendices
	certain items surplus to the scale allowed by the Equipment Detail available at HILSEA and the object of these surplus items was not clear. Eventually they were retained when the detachment marched out, in case of being required.	
HILSEA 19/10/14 1 pm	Orders received to join 8th Division at HURSLEY PARK near WINCHESTER.	8VD
HURSLEY 20/10/14 6 pm	Arrived at HURSLEY and were accommodated in SOUTH LYNCH CAMP.	
21/10/14 23/10/14 24/10/14	Attached to the Royal Artillery shewing with respect to the detachment, O.C. was handed two Equipment Details. That for 1 pr Q.F. Anti Aircraft gun, wagon, limbers, G.S. wagon attached to Div. Ammn. Colmn. being dated 6th October 1914 and the other being store carried with the Ammunition Park being dated	Routine Orders 8th Div 20.8.P

WAR DIARY
or
INTELLIGENCE SUMMARY.
(Erase heading not required.)

Army Form C. 2118.

Sheet 3

Hour, Date, Place	Summary of Events and Information	Remarks and References to Appendices
14th October 1914; Bott	Mobilization of this unit would have proceeded more smoothly if these details had been available at MILSEA – It was now seen that the apparently surplus stores referred to above were part (a very small part) of the stores ordered to be carried in the G.S. wagon. It was also noticed that the ammunition to be carried in the G.S. wagon with the Ammn Column was 1200 rds. instead of 2000. An indent was accordingly submitted for the additional stores allowed for the G.S. wagon, but there appeared to be some difficulty about the supply of them. The majority of them arrived, however, or were collected	being numbered 121/Stores/64. Appendix 1 consisting of telegrams on the subject

Army Form C. 2118.

Sheet 4

WAR DIARY
INTELLIGENCE SUMMARY.

Instructions regarding War Diaries and Intelligence Summaries are contained in F. S. Regs., Part II. and the Staff Manual respectively. Title pages will be prepared in manuscript.

Hour, Date, Place	Summary of Events and Information	Remarks and References to Appendices
HURSLEY 4/11/14	from the surplus of other units, and when the 8th Division received orders to embark the G.S. wagon, with 2 drivers and 4 horses, was handed over to the Div'l Amm'n Col'mn correct except for the Ammunition (1200 rds) and certain other items - chiefly spare brakegear S.B. and being attached. The Anti aircraft Detachment attached to H.Q. R.A. all movements from the 4th Oct to 9th Oct (embarkation etc) are as detailed in the WAR DIARY of H.Q. R.A.	S.B. S.B.
S'HAMPTON – LE HAVRE, per s.s.Tratton Hall		S.B. S.B.
LE HAVRE – MERVILLE per Rail		S.B.
LES LAURIERS near MERVILLE 9/11/14 1 p.m.	Arrived and billetted with H.Q. R.A.	
10/11/14 4 p.m.	The gun is ready for action - no aircraft sighted	
11/11/14	no aircraft sighted	
12/11/14	no aircraft sighted	
13/11/14	no aircraft sighted	

WAR DIARY
—or—
INTELLIGENCE SUMMARY.
(Erase heading not required.)

Army Form C. 2118.

Sheet 5

Hour, Date, Place	Summary of Events and Information	Remarks and References to Appendices
LES LAURIERS 10.20 p.m. 13/11/14	With reference to the remarks on the previous sheet that the S.A.A. wagon was handed over to the Div! Amm? (Colm?) I discovered this morning that it was parked with the 24th Field Ambulance I made inquiries and found that the Div? Amm. Col. had apparently repudiated all connection with this wagon, with the result that such matters as rations and forage, the men and horses were being cared for by no one - War Establishments (p. 44) that the wagon is attached to the Div. Am. Col. and I have now been once more handed over to them. At the same time the Ammunition has not been drawn. It would appear to me that a more	

Army Form C. 2118.

Sheet 6

WAR DIARY
or
INTELLIGENCE SUMMARY.
(Erase heading not required.)

Hour, Date, Place	Summary of Events and Information	Remarks and References to Appendices
	satisfactory result would have been obtained by following me of the following courses - (1) laid the wagon at an additional vehicle of the Rw. Am. Col. omitting all reference to it in the War Establishment of the Anti-Aircraft section (2) withdraw the wagon immediately with the gun and equipment to a gun inhow of mir at HILSEA &c... [See (1)]	
LES LAURIERS 14/11/14 10 am	Marched for MERVILLE en route for LA GORGUE	
LA GORGUE 14/11/14 1 pm	In billets at LA GORGUE - One tyre was broken on the way - a piece 14 inches long breaking away. It was buried in position with wires to	

WAR DIARY
or
INTELLIGENCE SUMMARY. Sheet 7

(Erase heading not required.)

Army Form C. 2118.

Hour, Date, Place	Summary of Events and Information	Remarks and References to Appendices
	protect the telling and the journey was completed without —	
LA GORGUE 5 p.m. 19/11/14	Marched out to take up a position at LE DRUMEZ near No 119 (H) Bty R.G.A. distance 2½ miles — Position (previously selected) reached — gun placed in position — digging of underground shelter and ammunition recess commenced — completed at 2 a.m. 20/11/14. The position has been chosen for extensive all-round view, but consequently lacks concealment — However the gun itself is disguised with straw, and if recognized as a gun, of sorts, might be taken for a dummy. Snow fell during the afternoon of the 19th and was followed by frost. No more snow falling to conceal the fresh earth, snow was carried	

WAR DIARY
INTELLIGENCE SUMMARY.
(Erase heading not required.)

Army Form C. 2118.

Sheet 8

Hour, Date, Place	Summary of Events and Information	Remarks and References to Appendices
	from elsewhere and scattered in such a way as to obtain concealment. The position is among some manure heaps and the shelters are placed in lieu of two of these for further disguise from view from above. It is hoped that the gun itself will be mistaken for a heap of straw or a cart loaded with straw. Sketches of shelters :— *[sketch: Shelter for Detachment, 8' wide, 5' and 2'3" marked]* *[sketch: Ammn. Recess, 4' wide, 2' marked]* 1 N.C.O. and 2 gunners are always with the gun	

Army Form C. 2118.

Sheet 9

WAR DIARY
or
INTELLIGENCE SUMMARY.
(Erase heading not required.)

Instructions regarding War Diaries and Intelligence Summaries are contained in F. S. Regs., Part II. and the Staff Manual respectively. Title pages will be prepared in manuscript.

Hour, Date, Place	Summary of Events and Information	Remarks and References to Appendices
LE DRUMEZ 20/11/14 12.45 p.m.	1 German aeroplane seen but out of range. not fired at.	MT
21/11/14 1.15 p.m.	A German aeroplane passed within easy range and was not seen by the n.c.o. on duty a most unfortunate piece of carelessness — Section officer was not far away and came up at once but was not in time to engage. Had the gun been even traversed in the right direction at the time when officer arrived, a belt of ammunition could have been fired — The following lessons were learnt from this most regrettable incident: — (a) When one machine is under observation (possibly a friendly machine) another man must keep a lookout in other directions — (b) Care must be taken that nothing prevents free and instant traversing in any	

Forms/C. 2118/11.

Army Form C. 2118.

Sheet 10

WAR DIARY
INTELLIGENCE SUMMARY
(Erase heading not required.)

Instructions regarding War Diaries and Intelligence Summaries are contained in F. S. Regs., Part II. and the Staff Manual respectively. Title pages will be prepared in manuscript.

Hour, Date, Place	Summary of Events and Information	Remarks and References to Appendices
	Inaction – (c) Failure to observe a hostile aircraft within easy range must be treated as gross neglect of duty.	
2 p.m.	Following message received :– S.C. 90 a.a. "Your ammunition has now been drawn in your wagon attached to 8th Div Amm" Col" This wagon will be attached to number 4 section D.A.C. Only 250 tracer shell instead of 300 were drawn" from 8th Div. Art?	850
5.30 pm	Under cover of darkness digging operations commenced to improve the underground shelter.	
9.30 pm	Shelter completed; now contains seats and fireplace.	GG.

WAR DIARY
INTELLIGENCE SUMMARY.
(Erase heading not required.)

Army Form C. 2118.

Sheet 11

Hour, Date, Place	Summary of Events and Information	Remarks and References to Appendices
LE TRUMEZ 22/11/14 10.40 a.m.	A German Aeroplane engaged and 8 rounds fired. No hits so far as could be judged - This target was not engaged as smartly as might have been - The N.C.O. on duty (not the same one as fired so noticeably yesterday) would have done better if he could. I have fired 2 or 3 belts of ammunition but see no practice. The total number allowed us for practice was only 50 rounds (2 belts) which is no doubt necessary on account of expense is miserably inadequate from the point of view of training (3. N.C.O's. of this detachment, to the duties to which can another be regarded as important. A. Shelmerdine)	

Army Form C. 2118.

Sheet 12

WAR DIARY
or
INTELLIGENCE SUMMARY.
(Erase heading not required.)

Instructions regarding War Diaries and Intelligence Summaries are contained in F. S. Regs., Part II. and the Staff Manual respectively. Title pages will be prepared in manuscript.

Hour, Date, Place	Summary of Events and Information	Remarks and References to Appendices
	I called both belts to be fired by the same N.C.O. and the improvement in his firing the second belt was extraordinarily noticeable. This convinces me that each N.C.O. or man who may have to act as numerer i.e. as a minimum, should fire at least 2 belts. If only the rounds can be got off at a good speed coupled with fair accuracy I am convinced that the correction of fire will not prove as difficult as is sometimes supposed and I expect this when the detachment has a little more experience, much of which could have been obtained at Shoeburyness	

Forms/C. 2118/11.

WAR DIARY
or
INTELLIGENCE SUMMARY.
(Erase heading not required.)

Army Form C. 2118.

Sheet 13

Hour, Date, Place	Summary of Events and Information	Remarks and References to Appendices
	with the expenditure of a few more rounds of this comparatively inexpensive ammunition.	
LE DRUMEZ 23/11/16 (Monday) 9.40 a.m.	A test having been left in the open all night in order to ascertain the effect of frost upon the tracer projectiles has just been examined. One tracer shell was unplugged and found that the liquid was unaffected. Today, the clouds being very low, no aircraft have been seen. Probably none were working.	K.D.
7.20 p.m.	This evening the gun has been shifted to a fresh position. Some boards having been found a platform has been laid on the ground, which is rather rough. This is an important point as it is essential that the gun be easily traversed in any direction. (See sheet 9)	

(9 29 6) W 2791 103,000 8/14 H W V Forms/C. 2118/11.

WAR DIARY

INTELLIGENCE SUMMARY. Sheet 14

Army Form C. 2118.

(Erase heading not required.)

Hour, Date, Place	Summary of Events and Information	Remarks and references to Appendices
	...ection. The new position is about 60 yds from the old one, so no new underground shelter is being constructed.	
	Two officers of the R.F.C. (M.W.) were here this afternoon and one of them gave me the following information:- (i) That an observer from the R.F.C. (M.W.) is allowed to each Anti Aircraft gun. (ii) That in at least one division the "bomb gun" has been relegated to the trenches. With regard to (i) such an observer seems likely to be of great use, and I.W.M. wrote in about it. As to (ii) if that is to be the fate of this gun I hope it will not be before we have had a fair trial at aircraft. J.L.	
LE DRUMEZ 24/11/14	Clouds very low no enemy aircraft seen today. O.O.	
-do- 25/11/14	Clouds low until about 3pm. when the weather	

WAR DIARY
INTELLIGENCE SUMMARY

Army Form C. 2118. Sheet 15

Hour, Date, Place	Summary of Events and Information	Remarks and references to Appendices
	cleared considerably. Several aircraft of the Allies were making flights but no German. With reference to the boards used as a platform these have not proved to be strong enough, but some stouter material having been obtained a really solid platform will now be constructed. We have received verbal orders to accompany No.119 (H) Bty, R.G.A. to a new position tomorrow. The new platform will accordingly be constructed there.	(Sheet 13)
LE DRUMEZ 26/1/14	Clouds low no chance of aeroplane observation. Marched off 2 p.m. to fresh billets on the road which runs N.W from ROUGE DE BOUT, and about ½ mile short of that place. Position selected in an orchard near two	2.10.

WAR DIARY
INTELLIGENCE SUMMARY.
(Erase heading not required.)

Army Form C. 2118.

Sheet 16

Hour, Date, Place	Summary of Events and Information	Remarks and references to Appendices
ROUGE DE BOOT 27/4/14 11 p.m.	circular hay-ricks. About 150 yards in right rear of 119 (H) Bty, R.G.A. Bright and clear. Much warmer. German biplane made repeated trips over our position. Fired at each time. 308 rounds fired at the same machine in the course of about an hour – but brought down – It was thought that two smoke balls were dropped by this machine to indicate position of 119 (H) Bty – but it is also suggested that these were two of our shells bursting in air – Reg¹ O.R.A. arrived and said that we were much too close to the battery and had given away the position of it – Ordered to move 800 yds away – Gun worked perfectly throughout and tracers clearly seen –	8¼ 8¼ 8¼

WAR DIARY
INTELLIGENCE SUMMARY.
(Erase heading not required.)

Army Form C. 2118.

Sheet 17

Hour, Date, Place	Summary of Events and Information	Remarks and references to Appendices
6.30 am 28/11/14	Moved to fresh position about B 25 c 2 b [Ref. Squared Map "Courtrai" S.W. of ARMENTIERES"] Platform laid and digging of underground shelter commenced —	

The fact that we fired 308 rounds yesterday without bringing down the machine is not conclusive that its gun is useless for anti-aircraft work, but only that something is wrong with the system of ranging, sequence of tracers and common etc —
The system upon which the belts have been

WAR DIARY
INTELLIGENCE SUMMARY.
(Erase heading not required.)

Army Form C. 2118.

Sheet 18

Hour, Date, Place	Summary of Events and Information	Remarks and references to Appendices

filled in as follows – T = Tracer C = Common
T T C C C C T C C C C T C C C C T C C C C
The layer is trained to fire the first 2 as single shots, pausing for the officer to correct as necessary, after which he goes to automatic and fires groups of 5. The object is to finish each group with a tracer upon which a correction can be made before the next group.
It now appears that owing to the vibration etc the 5th round of the group is the most erratically layed of the group. In fact the 1st round is probably the only correctly layed round of the group.
Experiments will now be made with belts filled in different manners. No opportunity

WAR DIARY

INTELLIGENCE SUMMARY.
(Erase heading not required.)

Army Form C. 2118.

Sheet 19

Hour, Date, Place	Summary of Events and Information	Remarks and references to Appendices
29/11/14	of firing occurred today but the most promising scheme seems to be to use tracer and common alternately and firing single shot laying afresh each time. Clouds low, bad for aeroplane observation. No enemy aircraft sighted.	S.S.O. S.S.O.
30/11/14 9.30 a.m	Clouds low today — Showery — unlikely weather for enemy aircraft. I have some belts filled as follows:— TTCCTCCTCCTCCTCCTCCTCC — These will be experimented with and another change in the system introduced, namely the layer will fire only single shots, getting a fresh lay each time, and (as before) making a pause for observation after each tracer. I wish to point out that	

Army Form C. 2118.

Sheet 20.

WAR DIARY
INTELLIGENCE SUMMARY.
(Erase heading not required.)

Hour, Date, Place	Summary of Events and Information	Remarks and references to Appendices
	If this system of belt filling (9 traces per belt) is to be better than that of 6 traces per belt it will show that a larger proportion of traces should be issued, as the number supplied on Mobilization only permitted 6 per belt and a few over, whilst the number drawn by Div Am Col only permits 5 per belt and a few over — With reference to the difficulties experienced on the 21st and 22nd flg have now arranged that the detachment does not do night guards so that a picket detachment are on duty all day — On the morning of the 20th it was found that some ice had formed in the water jacket. This was thawed and 2 pints of glycerine	

WAR DIARY
or
INTELLIGENCE SUMMARY.

(Erase heading not required.)

Army Form C. 2118.

Sheet 2 / 1

Hour, Date, Place	Summary of Events and Information	Remarks and references to Appendices
	added to the cooling water — also some straw fires round outside the canvas cover which I had made before leaving HURSLEY PARK	
5.30 pm	No enemy aircraft have been seen to-day. — No 12 1st Anti-Aircraft Section having arrived in the division this one is now known as the 1st Anti Aircraft Detachment 8th Division. 8Yd.	
	J. Moore Lt R a OC 1st Anti Aircraft per 8th Division	

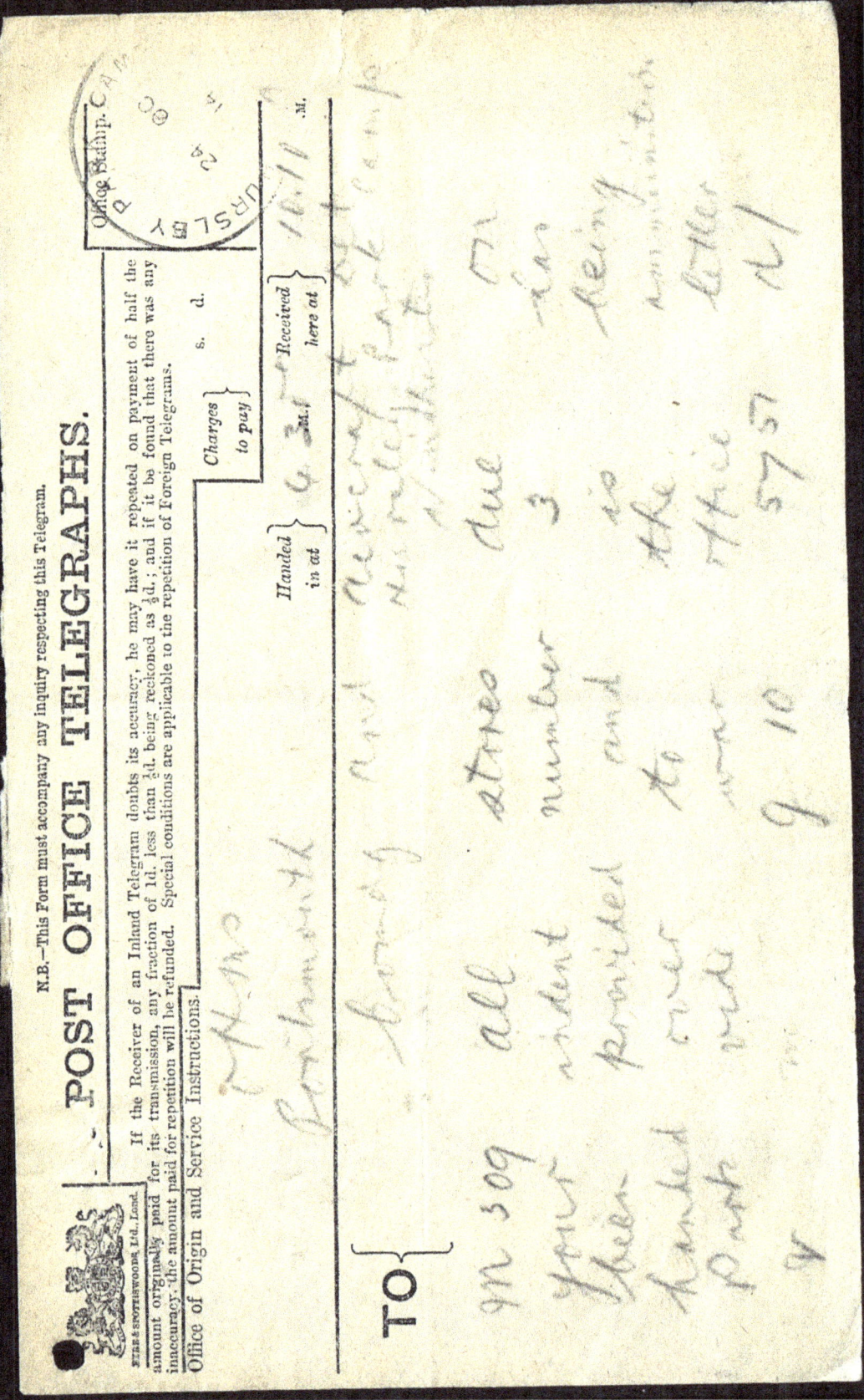

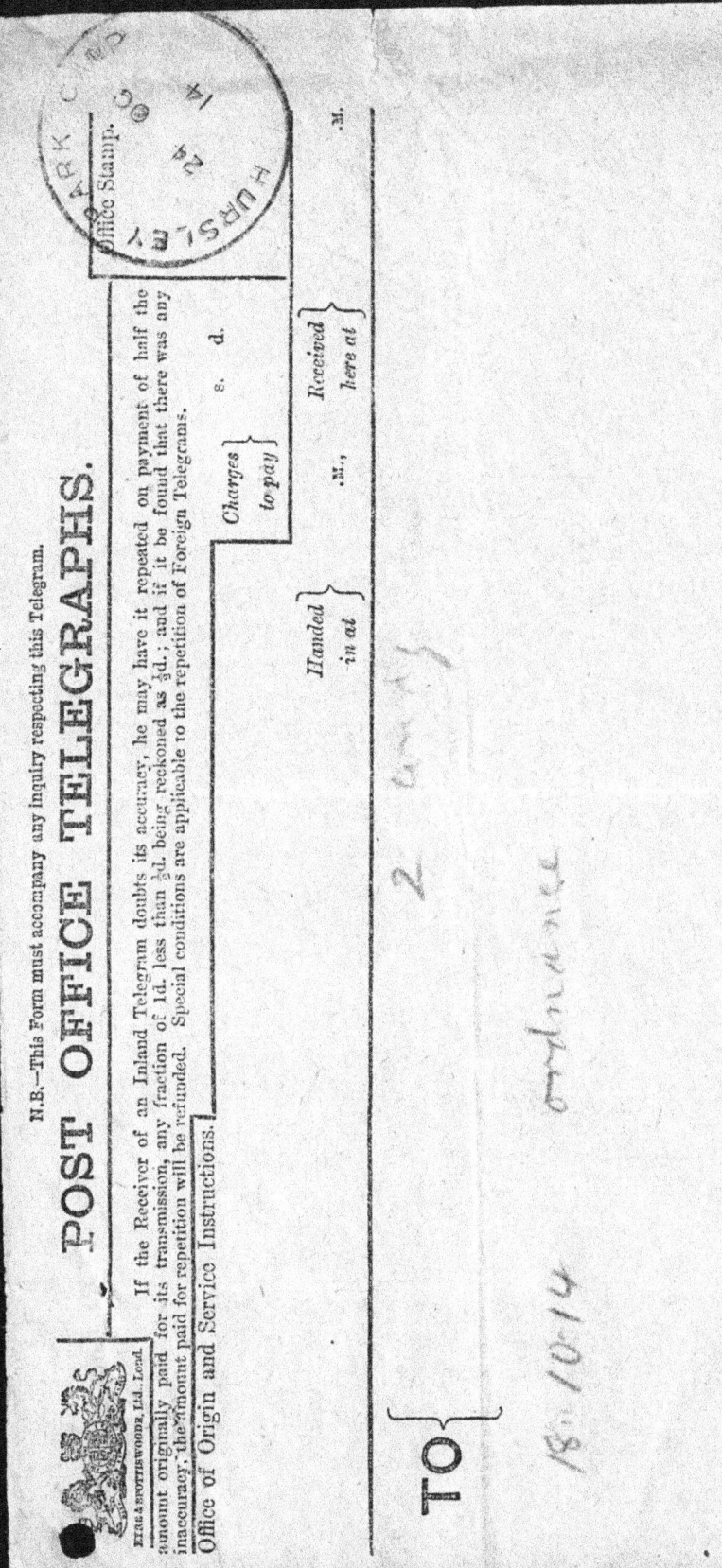

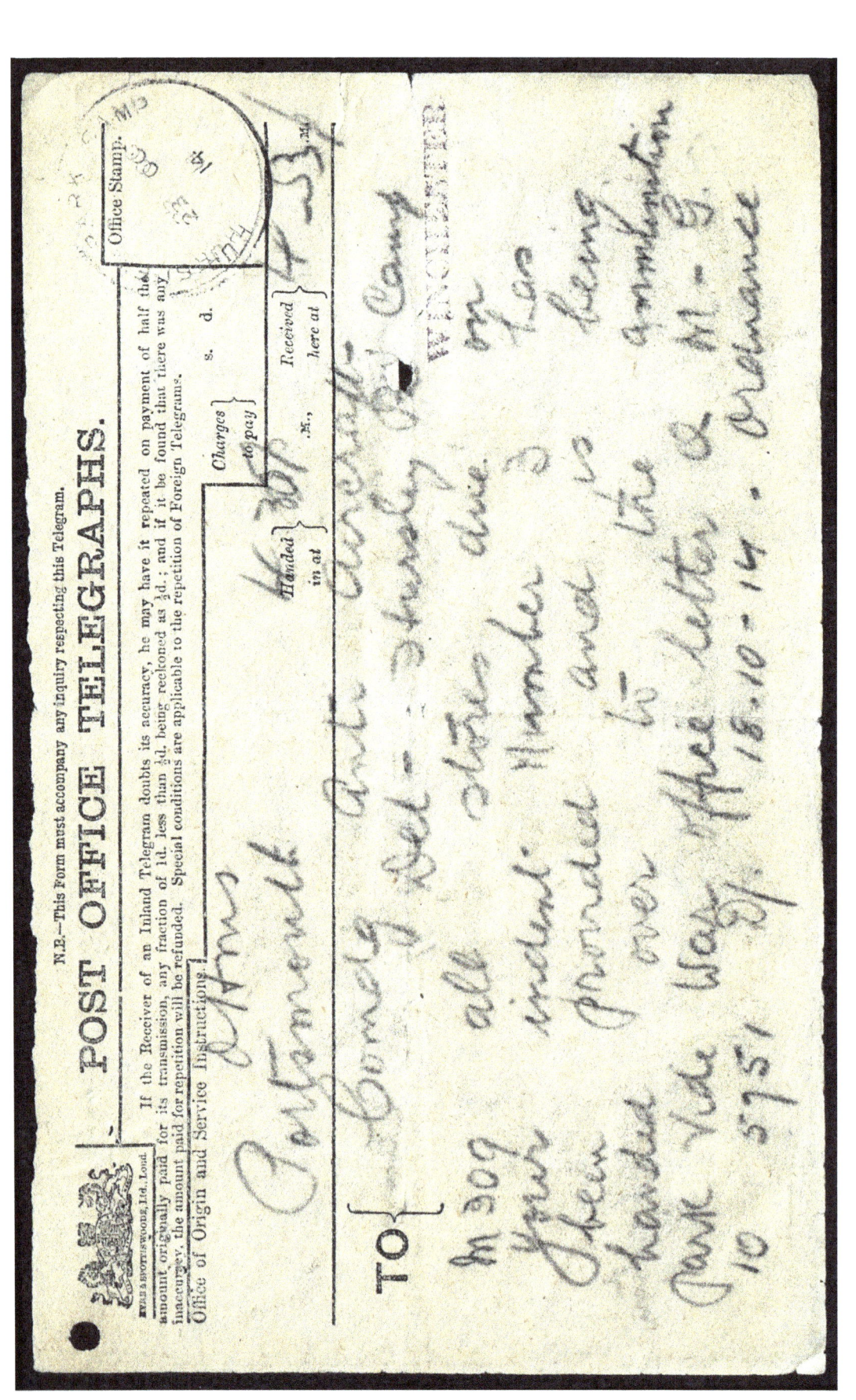

POST OFFICE TELEGRAPHS.

TO Mrs Postlethwaite

M 309 Gorney Anti aircraft your set-strictly confd. Green all stores due standard indent Number 3 handed provided and is over to the Southampton Park Vale Way Office letter G.M-G. 10 5751 SP. 18-10-14 - Ordnance

WINCHESTER

POST OFFICE TELEGRAPHS.

Office Stamp: CAMP / 30 OC 14

Handed in at 1.14

TO { Osborn
Portsmouth

Comdg Anti aircrafts det-
H. O. C.

M 254 your a 101 see
my five M 312 twenty third
mobi- table in
stores by given detail of
ammunition and spare parts
carried to

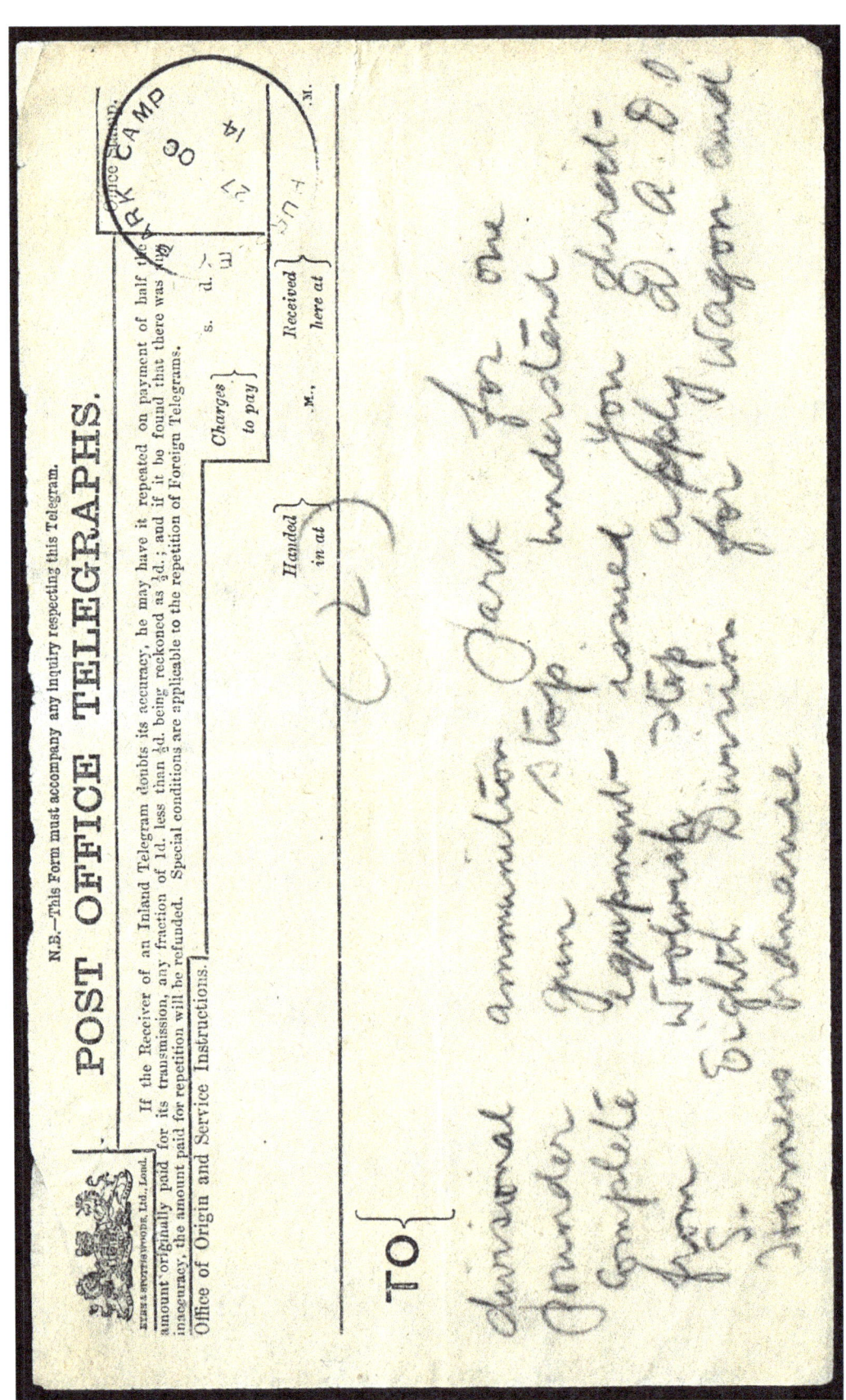

To:

General
Ordnance ammunition Park for one
complete gun equipment indent
from equipment issued for great-
S. eight Drivers coat apply D.A.D.
harness reference for wagon and

4 PM Friday

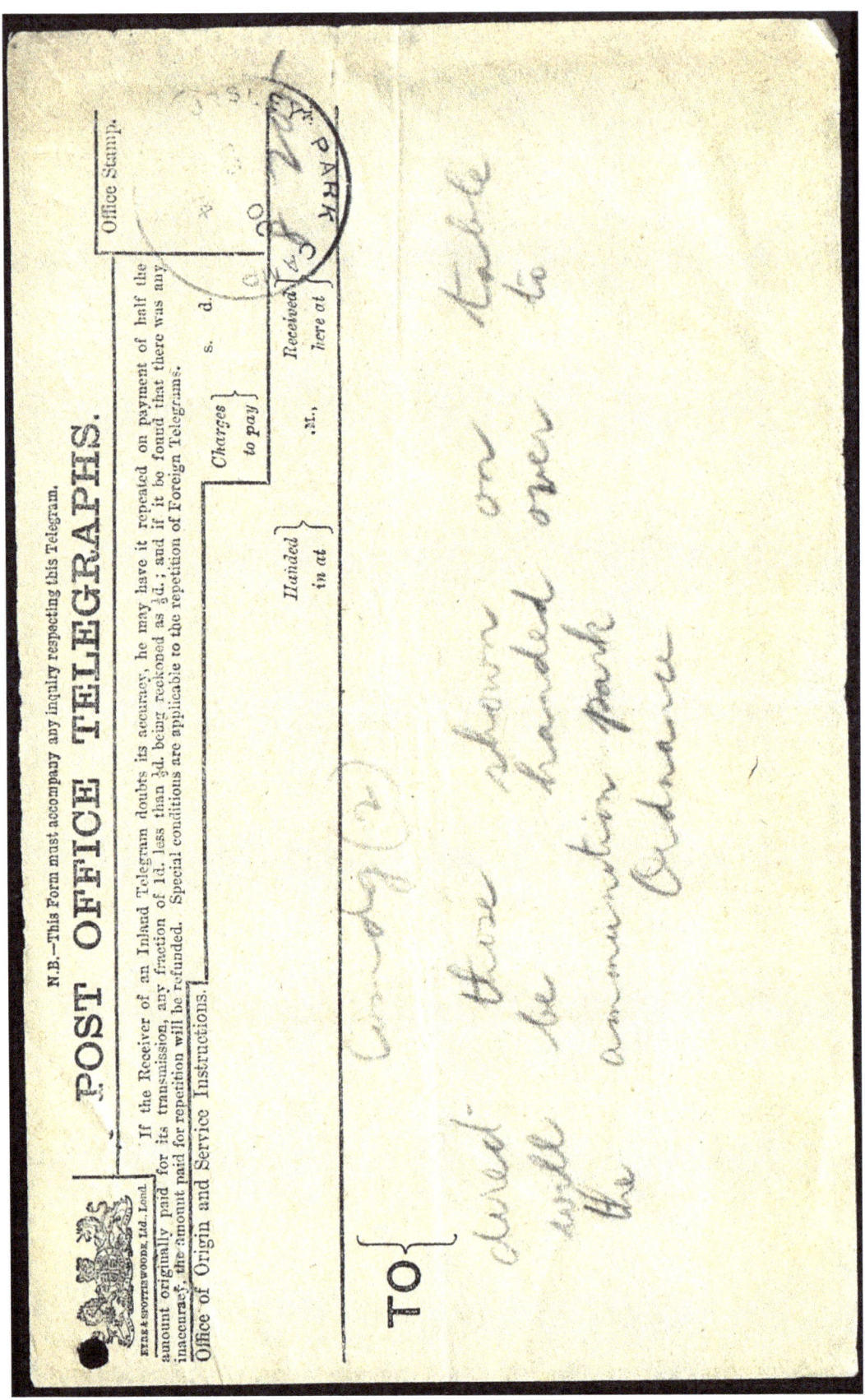

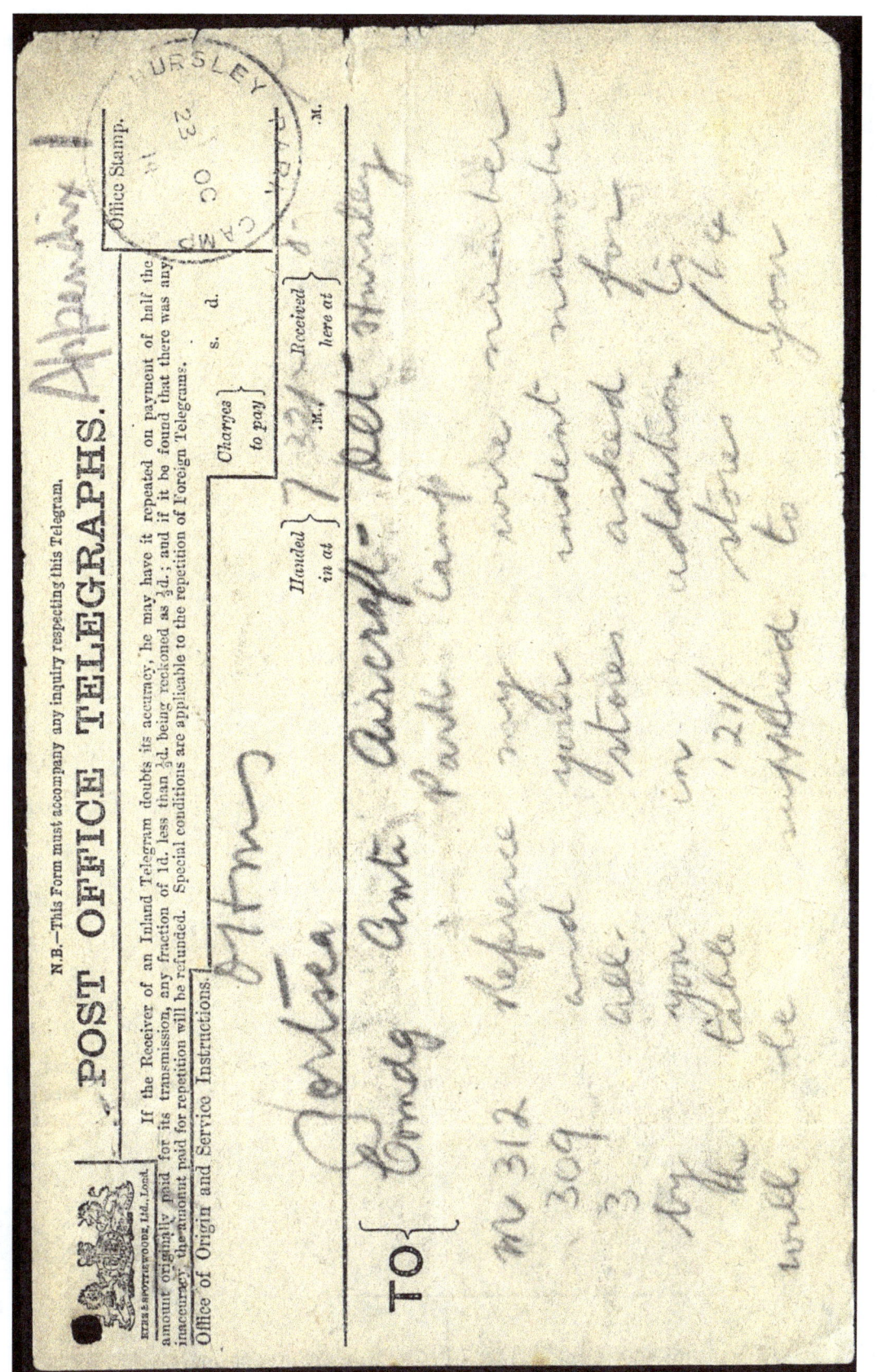

POST OFFICE TELEGRAPHS. Appendix

Office Stamp: HURSLEY 23 OC 14

Handed in at 7.24 Received here at

TO { Jones
Comdg Anti Aircraft All Hursley Park Camp

No 312
309 Reference my wire number
3 and your indent number
all fifteen asked for
by you in addition to
the Etha '21 stores
will be supplied to you

36

TO CONFIRM TELEGRAM.

N. W. O. Gosport

The following is a copy of a Telegram which was sent you this day, and is forwarded in confirmation. *[stamp: NAVAL STORE (MOBILIZATION) PORTSMOUTH]*

Handed in 10.40

TO {

27 10 14 19

M 252 Commanding Anti Aircraft Sunday field coup.
Your A. M. Lee my W.W. M.312 twenty third instant stop table 121 - stores
en. given details of ammunition stores and spare parts asked for and issued to Divisional Ammunition Park for one pounder gun

FROM {

TO CONFIRM TELEGRAM.

The following is a copy of a Telegram which was sent you this day, and is forwarded in confirmation.

_____ 19___

TO { 2nd Okus

OIF Unattached complete equipment reverse your direct form isolated stop apply D.A.D.O.S eighth division for wagon and horses

FROM { Ordnance

www.ingramcontent.com/pod-product-compliance
Lightning Source LLC
Chambersburg PA
CBHW080914230426
43667CB00015B/2677